CLOSING LEARNING GAPS

# NEW APPROACHES
# TO SUCCESS
# IN THE CLASSROOM

Norma Banas, M.Ed.                          I. H. Wills, M.S.

Illustrations by
Sharon Henderson

Cover Design
by
Steve Henry

**HUMANICS LEARNING**

**Humanics Learning**
PO Box 7400
Atlanta, GA 30357-0400

Library of Congress Card Catalog Number: 76-15126
ISBN 0-89334-323-4

# DEDICATION

Dedicated to all informed teachers who have been asking for ways to help make learning more successful.

# TABLE OF CONTENTS

# Introduction

# He Really Isn't Lazy

Some children do not receive and evaluate the messages of their sensory organs in the expected way, even though these organs may be unimpaired. These children are seen as very intelligent because they are very verbal, active and good with mechanical things. Kindergarten is probably a breeze for them, and the e are high expectations for above average school achievement when they enter first grade.

The easy progress through the pre-school level may suddenly come to a stop for some by mid-first grade. They cannot seem to learn to read, and recall of number facts is nil. Frustration sets in and is often followed by poor behavior. Our answer too often is, "He isn't motivated," or "He needs more discipline," or "He is just immature." None of these factors are probably the cause of the slowing rate of achievement. Children come to school eager to learn and expecting success. It is only after failure to achieve goals set by their parents, their teachers, or themselves that motivation wanes and effort decreases.

It is our job, therefore, to look at this child and identify his learning pattern of strengths, as well as weaknesses. We must look for any interferences in the physical development of the child that would affect learning; we must look at the perceptual (the ability of the brain to make meaning from what he sees, hears, or contacts); and we must check the ability to store and retrieve data sent to the brain. For full procedures on screening for learning interferences, see Banas and Wills, *Identifying Early Learning Gaps,* Humanics Limited, Atlanta, Georgia, 1975.

If visual, auditory, motor or neurological pathways show a deficit or lag in function, we must send the child to the appropriate specialist for an in-depth examination and for treatment. The learner must be free of functional interferences in order to use his intellectual potential and work to his ability level. Remember that these deficits may be subtle, and that lags or immaturities in the developing child may "go away with time," yet if we expect him to accomplish a skill while he is not equipped to handle that skill, we are setting up a failure syndrome which can follow him all through his life.

There are also students in our classrooms who are slower in overall development and who have less capacity for learning. It is often the case that these children are less capable because of the same perceptual or motor dysfunctions or lags in development, but to a greater degree. For them, it is a must that academics are presented almost entirely manipulatively and with the Associative Memory Aid. For a more detailed description of the learning interferences, behavior and needs of the slower learner, see Banas and Wills, *Success Begins with Understanding,* Academic Therapy Publications, San Rafael, Calif., 1972.

Others of our entering first graders may sail through first and even second grades with well equipped functioning vision, hearing and motor skills and good visual memory. However, third grade can suddenly seem very difficult, and progress starts to slow. The third grade curriculum changes the child from manuscript to cursive style. It moves him from addition and subtraction to multiplication. It has him read in books with often dramatically reduced type size and reduced open space between the lines (so visual skills must be well matured). It requires reading words, which no longer are simple in form and small in size, but are closely similar in configuration. Details become very important in rapid recognition (three, there, tree). If this is the first time any real problem is noted, a careful check of the perceptual areas of learning must be made. The *Frostig Tests of Visual Perception,* Marianne Frostig, Consulting Psychologists Press, Palo Alto, Calif., 1961, can be used by the classroom teacher and will yield developmental ages for five areas of visual perception directly needed in the reading process. *Identifying Early Learning Gaps* gives further symptoms and means of checking visual, motor, and auditory perceptual development.

Children with perceptual disorders or lags are referred to as having a "Learning Disability." The definition given to this syndrome is, ". . . a child of average or above average intellectual *potential* who manifests learning problems which are NOT due to physical handicap, visual, auditory or motor dysfunction, mental retardation, primary emotional disturbance, or environmental disadvantage."

Many doctors and educators feel that a learning disability is a developmental lag and that the child will outgrow his problems. To a degree this is true. Ideally, if we wait until age nine before we presented formal academics and work with symbols, we would see a dramatic reduction of learning problems. Unfortunately, our educational system does not provide the time for children to mature and become ready for skills but presents tasks at stages (grades) designed as appropriate for the average student at that level. The fact that the "average" may be a span of three years difference in readiness (both beyond and below the so-called average) to handle the designated task or skill has led teachers, parents, and the students to heights of frustration. It has led the educational system from one sure-fire approach to another, from open classrooms to team teaching to individualized programming to mainstreaming to . . .

Individual differences are acknowledged. Maturation is accepted as a reality of the interference in learning a task prior to the time of readiness. The methods presented in this book take into consideration the need to handle tasks before we may be fully ready to do so. There are three key approaches to success in the classroom: 1) kinesthetic (use of the body in exploring and learning about our environment; 2) manipulative (use of moveable materials to aid perceptual clarity) and 3) associative (the use of a clue attached to the symbol or abstract to give it meaning.) Eyes-closed experiences are included to build the ability to visualize, thus to build memory for reproductive tasks. Color coding and manipulative materials intensify and simplify stimuli as an aid in perception; thus accuracy of the initial learning experience is improved.

The approaches to teaching reading, writing, and arithmetic in this text are designed to be used in the classroom for the entire group or small groups, and can be used by any student for extra reinforcement as independent classroom work, or for home assignments that are individualized.

If a clinical program for the remediation of learning deficits and the development of learning readiness can be incorporated into the program, a fully comprehensive text is available for this purpose, authored by Banas and Wills and entitled, *Prescriptive Teaching: Theory into Practice,* Charles C. Thomas, Springfield, Ill., 1976. The approaches in this text are designed to help the students compensate for learning lags or deficits and to move forward through their strengths.

# Chapter I
# READY TO WRITE?

In order to handle the task of writing, the child must come equipped with well developed eye:hand coordination, the ability to see how the form is made, the ability to translate what he sees into a motor action, and with motor memory so he can reproduce, without a model, that which he has learned to copy. When a child has difficulty with the writing task, it is our job to break down the task and see which part is causing trouble.

The most easy to identify is poorly developed muscular control reflected in the inability to handle the writing implement, in difficulty cutting or tracing, in poor pencil or crayon grip, and/or in writing marked by tremorous or wavy lines.

1. Painting at an easel — from scribbling to finger painting, to brushed on watercolors — offers excellent writing preparedness. Kephart in *Slow Learner in the Classroom*, Columbus, Ohio, Charles Merrill, 2nd ed., 1971, offers many chalkboard or easel activities to develop gross motor control.

2. Coloring sheets with single or simple item pictures, such as provided by *Open Court Kindergarten Program*, "Perceptual Games," LaSalle, Ill., 1970, are on stiff paper, boldly outlined in a dark, thickened line to help the child notice limits. These pictures, or others taken from a commercially available coloring book and pasted on cardboard, can be traced, then cut out and repasted onto either stiff or regular paper according to the need. If cutting is a problem, provide stiff paper and lead the student through a progressive development: 1) cut along a crease, 2) cut fringe off the edge of a sheet, 3) cut along a straight bold, thick line, 4) cut with turns along a bold and thick line, 5) cut around curves on a bold and thick line, 6) reduce the intensity of the line, 7) reduce the thickness of the sheet of paper and repeat steps 1—6.

3. After the pictures have been traced, cut, and pasted to a new background, they are ready to be colored. They should be placed on a slant board or easel. To color, movements should be encouraged in a progressive fashion: 1) up and down movements, 2) horizontal movements, 3) diagonal movements, 4) then circular movements. Specific exercises using the entire arm and wrist can be designed and used as illustrated on a slant board, on easels, or at the upright chalkboard. It is inadvisable to move to small motor exercises, to lined paper, or to conventional table work until the child shows good control at the large motor level.

4. Small muscle control of the fingers and hand used in drawing and writing can be developed with a million and one grasp-release activities. Putting clothespins in milk bottles, putting chips in medicine bottles, counting pennies, playing with and making pictures with matchsticks, using a hole punch to punch out lots of dots, which are then pasted onto a form, as illustrated, to make a picture or a letter shape — all are excellent exercises for small muscle control. ALWAYS place the pieces to the left side of the container so the child learns to work consistently from left to right.

5. Initial drawing and writing experiences should be on large sized unlined paper on a slant board, as illustrated. The slanted surface is more desirable than working on a flat surface. Movements of the entire arm must be encouraged and the child is not to be allowed to rest his arm as he writes or draws.

In addition to muscle control, the child must have good visual:motor (eyes guiding arm, hand, leg, foot, etc.) perception and coordination. This can be observed in his ability or inability to stop and start his movements with pencil or crayon strokes from and to given points, to make lines meet, to integrate one form with another, or to see how the parts fit together to make a form.

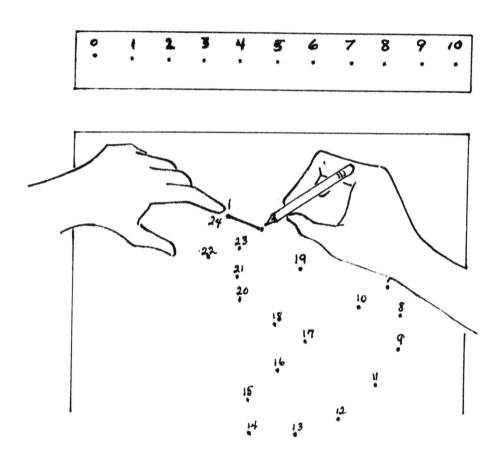

1. Dot-to-dot books can be used to help develop eye:hand coordination. Begin with simple designs with bold numbering or lettering. Teach the child to point with the finger of his non-writing hand to the dot to which he plans to move. This provides a visual goal which is concrete rather than linear. If control is poor, allow him to use a ruler at first to go from dot-to-dot.

Dot books also help the child see overviews from minimal clues. Play games guessing what the picture will be from as few connected dots as possible. If visual perception is very poor, the child may not recognize the picture until every dot is connected, and then only if it is a very clear and easy to recognize object. Others will be able to guess with a few connections.

If, following the number sequence is a problem, provide a conventional number line as a static visual referent (Key Card). This will also be beneficial in rapid sequencing awareness without having to return to the number one every time. It also will help him learn to recognize that the serial ordering of numbers beyond ten is the same as before ten.

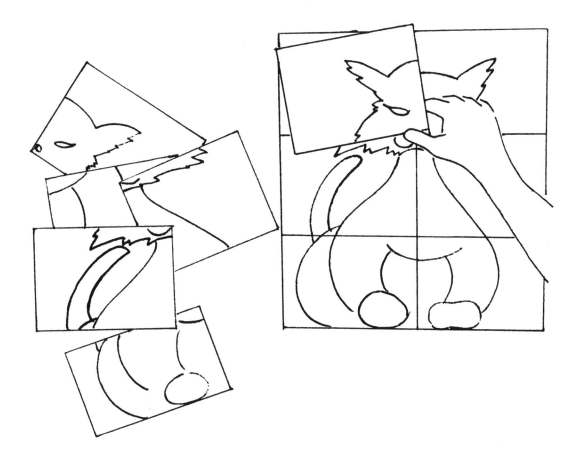

2. If a student does not seem to be able to integrate lines, see how forms are built from parts, or reproduce forms that he has learned to recognize, provide Coding Puzzles. To do this, you must have sets of pictures. Each set consists of two identical, simple line drawings — uncolored — as illustrated. One of the set is to be marked off into squares; the other of the set is to be cut into the same squares and becomes the puzzle. The marked model is placed in front of the child. The puzzle pieces are then placed to the left of the model, in random order, but each piece facing the student. The student MUST work from left to right and from the top left hand corner. "Look at the piece designated by this first square, (top left of model), find it among the puzzle pieces." The student must find the corresponding piece and, at first, may have to build his puzzle directly on top of the model. Later, he builds it at the right of his model until they fully match.

If the linear level is too difficult: 1) make sets of coding puzzles from full color pictures from magazines, 2) then make a linear model of the magazine picture (by tracing it), so that he matches the realistic to the linear representation, 3) then return to the linear match to the linear. For more uses of puzzles in the development of visual perception and visual memory, see Banas and Yelen, *Puzzle Power,* Humanics Press, Atlanta, Georgia, 1972.

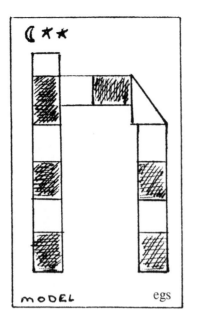

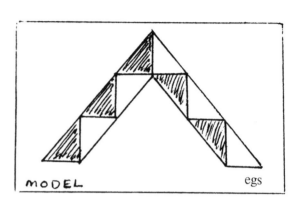

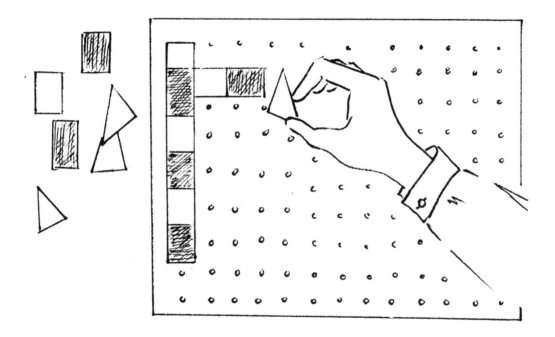

3.  Tile boards and tile pattern models offer another form of noting the details of form or letter formation. Commercially available tile sets with boards can be purchased at toy stores or school supply houses. However, it will be necessary to make models for the child to work to. Models should be made actual tile size as illustrated: 1) first in simple form without diagonals, 2) with diagnoal lines, 3) with crossing lines, 4) in letter shapes, and 5) in series of two to three letters properly spatially oriented.

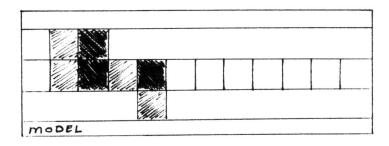

MODEL

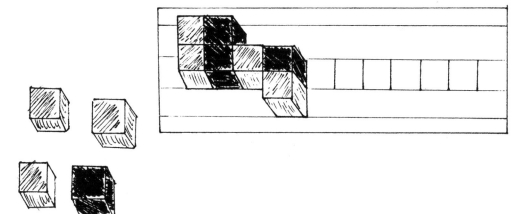

4. It is the spacing and spatial relations of letters in words that is often a problem in copying and writing. If this is noted, work with blocks and design cards, such as are available from Developmental Learning Materials, Chicago, Ill. (Pre-Writing Design Cards). These can be used to train the children to see relationships before they work at the linear reproduction (copy) level.

Some children learn to copy adequately, have good control, recognize the forms readily, and even learn to write (from memory) forms that they have practiced over and over again. It must be recognized that copying, and writing from recall are two distinctly different activities and tap different learning skills. If a child is noted to copy adequately, but is slow in writing from memory; or there is deterioration in form from memory, he needs training in motor memory.

To train motor memory, vision should be withdrawn from the training process. The theory is the same as learning to type; we must do so quickly and automatically without looking at our fingers or at the keys.

1. Kirshner's Body Alphabet, *Training That Makes Sense,* San Rafael, California, Academic Therapy Publications, 1972, provides an excellent program which uses the body in making the form of letters. We suggest that the children executie these forms, eyes closed. This makes it necessary to visualize without any clues.

2. Tile patterns, block patterns, and chalkboard exercises should also be followed by an eyes-closed reproduction step to insure transfer from copy to recall.

11

# Writing Readiness

Writing lessons at the linear level can often be more successful if accompanied by aids to motor control and visual accuracy. Clay, pipe cleaners, plastic letter sets and templates can provide the 3-dimensional form needed to develop control and detail accuracy. They are needed additionally because, though often a child can reproduce individual symbols accurately, his awareness of the relationship of one symbol to another is poor and causes him to reverse, transpose, or write illegibly.

Symbols should, therefore, be learned in combinations (in words). Symbols should always be learned in meaningful context.

Manuscript will lead to cursive. Because eye:hand control and directionality often are not well developed by the time cursive is needed for the writing task, the usual segmentation of letter forms is to be avoided in the print stage. If symbols are formed in a continuous movement, errors of directionality and control can be reduced. For example: "a" becomes $\alpha$ or $\phi$ when control problems interfere with accurate integration, because more than one movement is used. The directional confusion of letters, such as "b/d," can be lessened by teaching, "All letters are formed left to right, so "b" must be made $^x b$ and a "d" is $d$

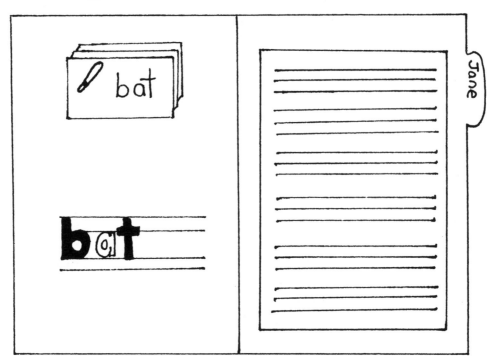

Materials: Manila folder for each child, ruled on the left flap for the placement of 2" plastic letters. A strip of colored cardboard glued to the writing line for kinesthetic and color clued baseline guide. – Plastic letter set (2") in lower case, with consonants in one color and vowels in another. – 3 x 5" unruled file cards to be ruled by the teacher for writing. Note writing line is to be darker than the rest.

Procedure:

    1. Child places a set of cards in the designated space at the top of the left flap of the file folder. (Begin with Set A.)

    2. Child then chooses the corresponding plastic letters to build the top word and places them, in sequence, working from left to right, as well as in correct spatial position. The picture is present to assure that this is a meaningful experience in vocabulary development, as well as for eye:hand control and visual perceptual accuracy.

    3. Child now copies the word on specially lined paper which he places on the right flap of the file folder. (Some children might need to have their model above at first.) Regular primer paper should be avoided as the lines tend to confuse.

    4. Continue through a set, building each word, then copying it under the other words on the special paper.

    When phonics and spelling skills are being developed, the child should progress to Set B. He places the picture sides up, forms the word with his letter set, and checks for correctness before copying the word to the paper. Set C. requires the child to be aware of the spatial orientation and translate it to his written form with no guide lines. This helps increase space awareness.

    5. Cards can be stored in a vocabulary box (3x5" file box) for use this and other ways.

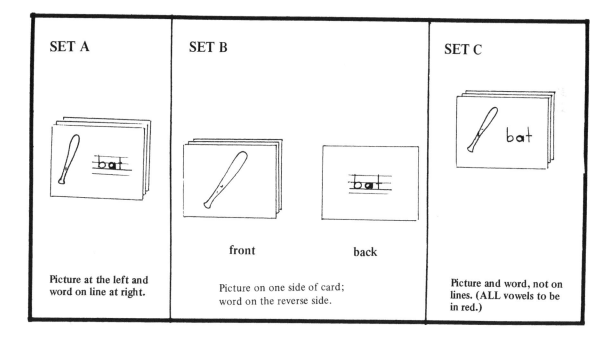

| SET A | SET B | SET C |
|---|---|---|
| | front      back | |
| **Picture at the left and word on line at right.** | Picture on one side of card; word on the reverse side. | **Picture and word, not on lines. (ALL vowels to be in red.)** |

Lined paper, as illustrated, with spaces between every three lines.

# "Associa - Pictograms"[1]
# The Print Stage

# K through 2nd Grade

Copying and writing letters or words several times is a common classroom practice. Unfortunately, children with perceptual, motor, or attention deficits tend to copy incorrectly; or they may copy accurately at first, only to lose details and accuracy on subsequent rewrites. Since this causes reinforcement of errors, it is not a desirable activity.

Tracing has long been used as an alternate to increase accuracy and awareness of the shape and the details of letters and words. By tracing over an original there is less chance of errors.

For many, tracing alone has not effected recall to a sufficient degree, especially for the abstract symbols and words of our language. A pictogram step (picture illustrating the meaning of the word) added to the familiar VAKT (visual:auditory:kinesthetic:tactile) method is the ASSOCIATIVE link to boost recall for symbols. By the addition of a meaningful picture clue, not only is the recognition of the symbol improved, but meaning is more accurately developed and lessons in handwriting become lessons in learning to read, to write, to spell, and to give meaning to words. The addition of the Associative link was introduced by Mrs. Frances McGlannan at the McGlannan School, in Miami, Florida.

Letters are best taught in context (in words) and NOT in isolation. It is the space/size relationship and the sequencing of the symbols that causes trouble for children with perceptual, motor, or attention problems.

In addition, the segmented or ball and stick methods of teaching writing are very difficult for children with lags in motor or eye:hand coordination and perception. A change to continuous line movements of the Non-segmented Alphabet as illustrated, can alleviate this problem and set the stage for the later transfer to cursive, which requires the habit of smooth left to right joined movements.

Some children cannot transfer what they learn in an isolated and structured exercise. Some can handle single elements and repetitive copy, but cannot shift constantly from one symbol and sequence of symbols to another. Therefore, writing lessons should always be with words.

(1) This section is reprinted with modification, by permission of Charles C. Thomas, Publishers. *PRESCRIPTIVE TEACHING: Theory into Practice,* Banas and Wills, 1976.

15

| incorrect | | correct |
|---|---|---|
| dOg | **SIZE: SPACE PROBLEM** | dog |
| Went | | went |
| PaPer | | paper |
| φpe | **VISUAL: MOTOR LAG** | ape |
| xyφʃ | | was |
| φϼϼ | **DIRECTIONALITY ERRORS** | bag |
| saw | | was |
| Pи๐ɹ | | PauL |

16

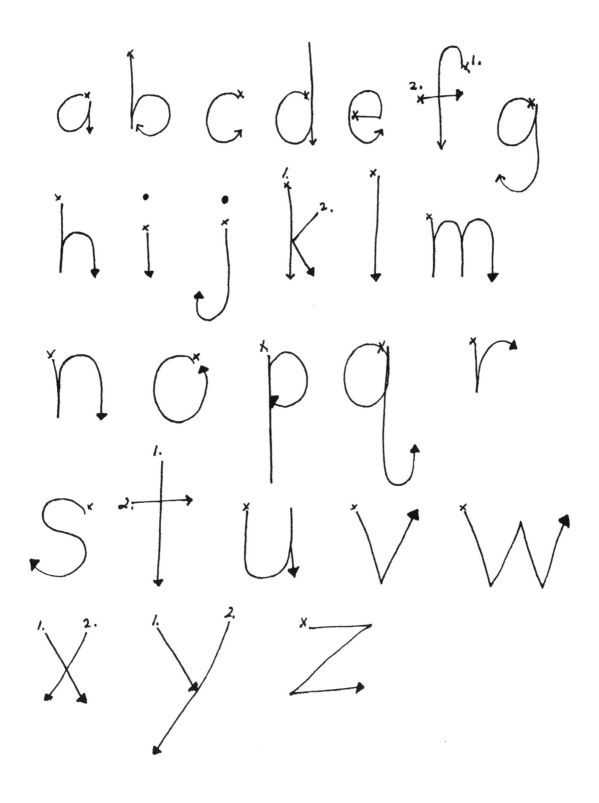

# incorrect      correct

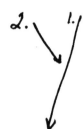 

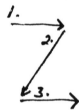

<u>Materials</u>:
8½ x 11" sheet of newsprint or unlined paper
red pencil
black grease marking crayon

<u>Procedure</u>:
Clearly print a word on the board, being certain to provide bold, correctly formed and correctly spaced letters. Use letters in words the child currently needs and will use daily.
<u>Step I</u>. Teach the child to copy, with his red pencil or crayon, on the 8½ x 11" sheet. Teach him to observe accuracy of spacing, of size, and of movement from top to bottom, left to right.

Remember that the children with slower developing <u>eye:hand control</u> may make many errors with a conventional segmented form of printing. These errors virtually disappear when letters are formed in a continuous movement (see alphabet chart).

Children with poor directionality awareness and habits MUST form symbols properly left-to-right, top to bottom, or their transfer to cursive will be difficult. Thus, the "ball and stick" approach is to be discarded.

Have him use his finger, if needed, to keep his (imaginary) line level as he moves from one letter to the next. If control or perception is very poor, the teacher should print the word on his sheet for him (or provide dittoed sheets ready for classroom use).

Do NOT use lined paper. The student then becomes reliant upon the meeting of his letter with top and bottom line and does not attend to the space:size needs or to the spatial relationship with its fellow letters. They also learn writing as a visual skill rather than a motor skill. Writing should be through automatic motor memory, as needed in typing or driving a car, or it will remain slow and require attention to the paper instead of to the material being copied.

<u>Step II.</u> With guidance from the teacher, the children think about the word and draw a picture to express its meaning. The picture must be placed at the top of the paper.

Pictures must accurately express the meaning of the word. The drawing quality is of no importance, except that you and the child can tell what is expressed. The children should be taught to use stick figures as much as possible. (See illustration page 21.)

Pictograms should show "who or what is involved" (nouns are generally no problem to picture), "Where is he (it)?" and an action, "What is he (it) doing?" This guide helps the students develop accurate definitions and organized thinking.

Be careful that stereotypes or vague definitions are corrected through accurate pictures. (See illustration page 22.)

# PICTOGRAM SAMPLE

girl   boy
woman   man

animals
cat   dog   cow

tree   flower

go

run

think

speak – say

day   night

time

state
city   city

country

house   church   school

happy   sad   scared

on

over

under

$+$ = and

$-$ = but

minute          minute

borrow          borrow

winter          winter

aunt          aunt

<u>Step III</u>. The children now are asked to trace their word 3 times with a fat crayon *while* saying the whole word. They should concentrate on the total word during the tracing. (Many young or problem learners will stop and talk in the process, will try to say each letter, or will trace each letter 3 times). Directionality must be carefully watched and correctly enforced. An arrow may be needed by some problem circular letters, such as "a", "o", etc.

<u>Step IV</u>. Children then turn their paper over and write the word (WITH EYES CLOSED), on individual desk, chalkboard, or another piece of newsprint. DO NOT let them "get a final look" before writing with eyes closed, as this would imply use of visual memory. This is to be discouraged by immediate turning over of the paper after tracing.

Children MUST check their own work. Turn the card over, "Is it correct?" If they falter or are inaccurate, they must return to the tracing step until they can write the word from recalling the feel of the movement.

<u>Step V.</u> Two to three new words a day should be introduced, depending upon the grade level. The word sheets should then be filed in a manila folder or notebook and be reviewed at the end of each week as an EYES-CLOSED spelling:writing test. Recall of the meaning of each word can be checked by asking the children to add a pictogram next to each word (from memory) on his test sheet. Words that are recalled with ease can be "tossed away" dramatically to build a feeling of achievement.

# "Kina - Writing" [2]

## The Cursive Step
## Grade 3 Up

The key to writing and reading cursive is the establishment of an association between the printed and the cursive form. Cursive is, in reality, print connected. Only 4 symbols change from the manuscript form (not including capital letters). Through a step-by-step kinesthetic:associative approach, the child should learn to conceptualize and visualize the cursive process *as the printed form connected.*

*Always* teach cursive using words; never teach or practice letters in isolation.

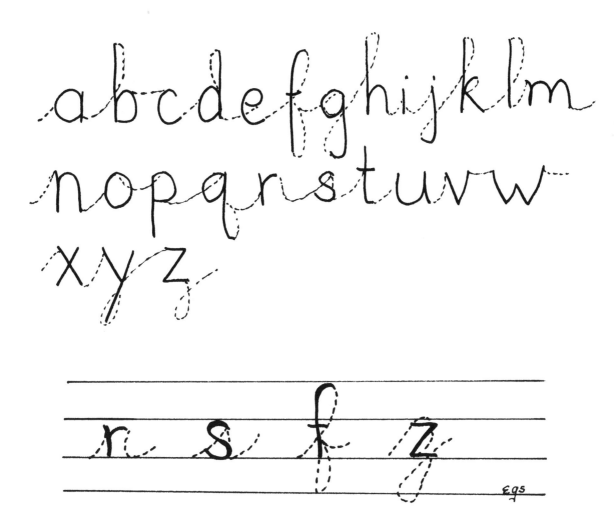

(2) This section is reprinted with modification, by permission of Charles C. Thomas, Publishers, *PRESCRIPTIVE TEACHING: Theory into Practice,* Banas and Wills, 1976. Kina-writing was developed and named by the authors and has been used at Educational Guidance Services, Inc. with success since 1967.

<u>Materials</u>: 4½ x 11" strips of white, unlined tagboard (hereafter called kina-cards)

 grease marking crayon

 red pencil

<u>Procedure</u>: Take words from any book in which the child is working which requires reinforcement. At first, avoid words with an r, s, f or z. These are the letters which change from the printed form to the cursive form.

<u>Step I.</u> COPY *in print,* one word each to a kina-card, in red pencil. Proper and exaggerated spatial relations are needed to fully involve the child kinesthetically and to heighten his perception of the shape and details of the word. Copy no more than five words per lesson. Check for accuracy of copy and proper letter formation and spacing.

Follow the same principles of non-segmented printed form and left-to-right, top to bottom movements as described in Associa-Pictograms.

front

<u>Step II.</u> DRAW A PICTURE on the back of each card to illustrate the meaning of the word. Teacher or parent must check at first for correctness and accuracy of meaning. Thinking, "Who, What, When, Where, Why, How" helps the student make his pictogram fully meaning-ful. Keep pictogram simple, but accurate. Discourage extraneous details which are not needed to provide meaning.

The associative pictogram aids recall of sight vocabulary, of spelling, of meaning vocabulary, and of foreign language vocabulary.

back

Step III. CONNECT each letter, using the crayon, so the finished word appears in cursive form. (At first, teacher illustrates on the board using 2 chalk colors). Careful guidance is needed at this step, where directionality and eye:hand coordination problems may interfere with the child's execution.

The instructions given in introducing the connective step are: "Swing up to where the letter begins when you print "s". (Note that it is often necessary to guide the child's directionality awareness by placing an arrow to remind him that all letters move from left to right as they are formed, and that we begin at the top of each letter.) ". . . make your letter just as you have been doing (in manuscript), *s* swing up to the next letter *sl* , make that letter, *sl* . ., etc."

front

<u>Step IV</u>. TRACE a word *3 times,* with the crayon *as* the student says the word quietly, *but aloud.* (Be sure he keeps his arm from resting on the table. Freedom of movement as well as large movements is important.) Then, turn the card over and WRITE the word on the chalkboard or scrap paper with EYES CLOSED. *Check to the model. Retrace if incorrect.* Do each word in turn.

<u>Step V.</u> FILE words in a shoe box, in abc order, for use as flash cards and vocabulary and spelling builders review. About every two weeks have students "test" each other by calling off the words from the box and writing them, eyes closed. All words written correctly are discarded. Words still difficult should be reviewed for appropriateness and/or given in another format.

PICTOGRAMS as a memory boost must be done properly to be of benefit. The key to recall may be the vivid or even unique association, in picture form, which is brought to the word *by the child.* The clue *must be his* clue. The association must be meaningful to him. With words which are easily visualized and concrete and which he can learn through a phonetic analysis approach, this method may be time consuming without sufficient benefit. To use it with words which are less tangible makes the child search for a key to open the door to recall. Once HE opens the door by finding the proper key, he will be more likely to remember how, the next time he approaches it. If we open the door for him, how will he know how to do so himself the next time?

EYES-CLOSED WRITING requires a true internalizing of the feel of the form and the movement and is a MUST. Children must not be allowed to look back at the word after tracing, as they are then using immediate visual imagery instead of motor memory. Motor memory requires concentration which intensifies intake. Eyes-closed (or look away) writing, instead of conventional "watch the line," is essential for speed. You cannot use writing for note taking or communication if the penmanship is taught as a visual skill.

# Copy Speed and Accuracy

The end product of learning to write is communication. We do this in several ways. First, we receive information from the written form (reading). To do this we must be able to recognize individual forms, recognize the serial order which tells us the specific sound or meaning to put to the forms, and must do this regardless of the tremendous variety or manner of presentation (style) of the form. Not only must we read at times from printed and at times from cursive style, but we must recognize letters and words in many varieties of printed and cursive forms. Each teacher has her own way of forming symbols, and not always exactly as we may have learned the form. This lack of form constancy can be a serious problem to children with a lag or deficit in visual perception.

In addition, if visual skills are not operating efficiently, we may find that we cannot readily recognize forms or keep our place in viewing series of forms when they are in small type, on cluttered papers, on purple inked dittos, at the board instead of at our desk, or embedded in context as opposed to in isolation, as on flash cards.

Secondly, we must translate what we see into a motor movement in a copying activity. The skills necessary for this have been covered in the beginning of this chapter.

Third, we must reproduce from memory, the written symbols, and communicate information using the specific serial order of our language code. In order to write (using this term to mean "communicate information"), we must recall the symbol needed and the proper sequencing of symbols within a word (spelling), and we must sequence words in a specific (grammatical) order. Visual and motor memory are required, as well as all the previously discussed readiness skills. If students exhibit inaccuracy in the copy or writing tasks, yet have good visual and motor control and perception, training will be needed in MEMORY.

1. The first requisite to develop memory is *visual attention.* Not only must he be able to concentrate on the task at hand, but he must be able to focus his vision on a specific place, be able to keep his place, look away and return to that place, and hold the visual image until he can reproduce it in written form. Verbalizing (talking aloud to himself) has been found extremely valuable in aiding attention span and helping memory. Verbalizing is a MUST for children with memory problems.

2. Placement and format of the copy is important to visual accuracy and should be presented in the following stages: 1) initially, place copy at the top of the student's work area. Be sure it is in bold, dark type, on uncluttered paper, and there is a great deal of white space between lines and words. 2) Reduce type size and line intensity and space between lines gradually. 3) Place copy material at the left (NEVER to the right of the work paper). Next, 4) when copy is accurate at the desk, move it further away from the student until gradually the child is copying from the board. Be sure the copy is clear, bold, and spaced for case of keeping his place.

Material to be copied should be two or three simple word *phrases,* then longer phrases until the level needed by the student is reached. Words should be of a simple nature at first, then incorporate easily confused words and irregular words, then numbers, abbreviations and punctuation.

3.  Goal setting is also important in developing good writing skills. We must be careful to develop writing skills for the *purpose of speed and accuracy in communication* and not place undue emphasis on penmanship for the sake of penmanship.

Unlined writing paper should be provided as the child should be using motor memory and NOT be looking at the lines on his paper.

Large size writing should be encouraged at first in speed copy activities. Size reduction can be allowed when motor memory and visual accuracy is adequate. Crossing out an error is preferable to erasing. Children should never be allowed to start all over when they make a single error. (Later they should learn to work in rough draft and follow that with a finished corrected paper).

4.  Self-checking is an essential aspect of copy accuracy. Begin from the very first copying activity. At first, tell the student that there is an error and where (but do not tell what the error is). Later, tell that there is x number of errors, but do not designate where they are to be found. Great pride can be evoked when children learn to find and correct their own errors. (Requesting error-free initial copy would be like asking us to never make mistakes). It is realistic to make mistakes, but we must be able to catch our errors and correct them. This should be a major goal in copying and writing lessons.

5.  Cursive style is preferable to manuscript for children with perceptual, motor and/or directionality deficits or lags, and once a child has been taught cursive, he should not be allowed to fall back into the use of the manuscript form.   ·

T hec ati sont heb ox.

Even if space control between symbols remains uneven, the connected style assures that we *and he* can read what he wrote.

Thecatisonthebox.

30

# Chapter II
# LEARNING BY DOING

Basic Principles for Teaching Language Arts

The ability to spell, read, and write depends upon the development of the ability to analyze the parts and see how they fit into the whole, and to automatically recognize and recall repeated stimuli. Both a phonetic analysis approach and sight recognition should be provided each child.

To learn these skills the student will need:

a) accurate visual and auditory discrimination (ability to see and hear likeness and differences between forms

b) good visual and auditory perception (making meaning from what he sees and hears)

c) reliable visual and auditory memory (both recognition recall and the ability to obtain an image in the mind)

d) the ability to reproduce (in writing or speech) what is viewed or heard.

Most important when working with symbols, and most troublesome to many children, is the need for automatic and consistent left-right directional habits. Words are but a series of symbols whose sounds are designated by their placement in relationship to each other. A change in the relations of the symbols within a word will alter the meaning of the symbols and of the word. Thus, "was" becomes "saw," "first" is "frist," or "there" becomes "three." Many individual letters do not have a constant sound; the sound is determined by the letter placed near it. (cap, cape, wait, draw, tall, Paul, warm, car). Thus, symbols should *always be taught in context.*

DIRECTIONALITY, for many, can be the key to spelling, reading and writing success. Children usually do not have an awareness of the need for a consistent left-right viewing pattern when they enter formal school age. Too many children do not seem to gain this, even after considerable schooling, and directional errors plague all their efforts. Directional errors in forming symbols are statistically not supposed to be significant until after age nine, but school does not wait for the slower maturing child, but expects all children to learn tasks requiring accurate and automatic directional awareness from age six or seven.

A directional arrow placed at the top left of each page can serve as a concrete reminder to view from left to right. Of course, clinical training in eye movement, tracking, and scanning, as well as development of laterality (the internal awareness of the two-sidedness of our body) and dominance (the establishment of one side of our body as the consistent lead side in all activities) may be needed before these children can do more than just learn to compensate for lack of inate directional sense.

MANIPULATIVE materials can increase awareness and accuracy for details for directionality and for sequence, as it provides a step between what the eye sees or the mind recalls and what the hand writes or copies. A lag in development of visual perception (making meaning from what is seen) can cause children to appear to make so-called "careless" errors when working in context as opposed to viewing work in isolation. This is because the proper position or relationship to other details is inconsistent. Omissions, additions and changes of positions are common errors corrected by manipulative materials. Manipulative materials help the student see the vital parts of a word, as he physically experiences the structure, rather than sees just mentally or visually.

This chapter introduces and suggests uses for a letter tray, a letter box, alphabet boxes, and a language box for individualized or group programs in reading and spelling, where manipulation is needed to help students compensate for readiness gaps or deficits in visual or auditory perception. Independent, fun-type manipulative reinforcement is offered through new uses of Go Fish and Concentration games.

Spelling and reading vocabulary has been traditionally taught as a visual-auditory (look-say) activity and remedially taught as a visual-auditory-KINESTHETIC (look-say-write or trace) activity. It has been noted in clinical schools that children who learn to read through a KINESTHETIC approach, using tracing and eyes-closed recall, are more able to write and to spell, as well as improve in sight reading accuracy.

Samples of typical exercises from workbooks show how the kinesthetic technique should replace the conventional instructions of "cross through," "circle" etc., which is testing, not teaching.

Note how the tracing of the symbol establishes a motor pattern and heightens the visual match.

• Recognition here is reinforced by copying and by using the whole word approach.

The rhyming elements are learned by combining sight recognition with tracing.

The kinesthetic (tracing) step reinforces the recognition of rhyming elements. These words may be recopied and an Associative Picture drawn next to each word to insure accurate interpretation.

| | | | |
|---|---|---|---|
| m**en** | cot | fi**x** | m**ass** |
| t**en** | f**a**t | mi**x** | miss |
| tin | r**a**t | max | l**a**ss |

Blends must be recalled by combining auditory and visual. Note the reinforcement of the whole by tracing the entire word.

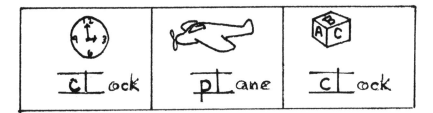

Choice or completion exercises must be combined with picture clue and tracing of the whole word. A model for matching is essential to avoid guessing.

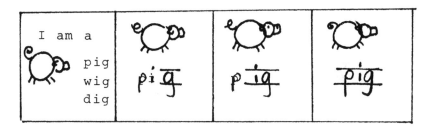

I am a
pig
wig
dig

This change of approach offers positive, error-free practice toward developing accurate recall with any or all subjects being learned

AUDITORY REINFORCEMENT (talking aloud) is another form of active involvement for children who have a visual, perceptual or attention deficit. It is not sufficient for many children to see and write a word only. They must reinforce the sound/symbol association through the auditory pathway as they repeat the word *while seeing or writing it.* It is the combination of auditory-visual-kinesthetic reinforcement in the one instance that bombards the sensory pathways and aids in attention, thus recall. This easy to follow technique should be required during all tasks where attention and accuracy are important.

There is a need for REPRODUCTION WITH EYES CLOSED as part of the kinesthetic experience to insure the accuracy at intake. The ability to write – in addition to being a motor skill – is the ability to bring forth, *automatically,* the written symbols for a word. Instruction in spelling and writing should never be an isolated activity. Spelling and writing are needed simultaneously, if either is to be effective. Following directions accurately requires interpreting what was heard or read. Until the student tries to execute an activity, we, nor he, do not know if the instructions were understood. Thus, *immediate* response by trying an activity or a problem tells us a great deal about intake accuracy. Our first instruction while presenting a lesson should be, "Try with me as you listen."

Recently, the importance of bringing meaning to symbols has increased the awareness of, and the use of, the ASSOCIATIVE CLUE (meaning given to a symbol or abstract) as a major memory aid. Recognition memory comes before recall or reproduction memory, and reading may be accomplished with minimal clues; but spelling, match, and writing must be accurate for every form and detail. The use of picture clues is illustrated and should be used with all subjects, especially on initial presentation of a new concept, rule or skill.

Rules for vowel sounds, for grammar, for syllabification, and for structural analysis are often arbitrary ones. Our language code is inconsistent at best. The Associative Approach attaches a meaning clue to aid recall and is essential for many children.

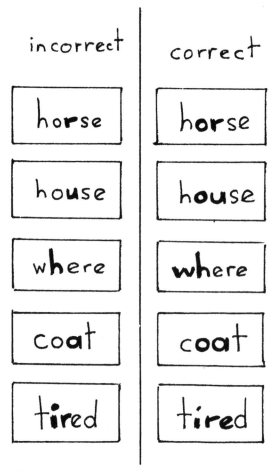

Color clues can be used for intensification of pertinent parts and/or as an association for the unit being empha-sized. Color clueing must be used properly and carefully so that an accurate visual association is made.

# ASSOCIATIVE ALPHABET TRAY

## Kindergarten & 1st Grade

**VISUAL AND AUDITORY SEQUENCE**

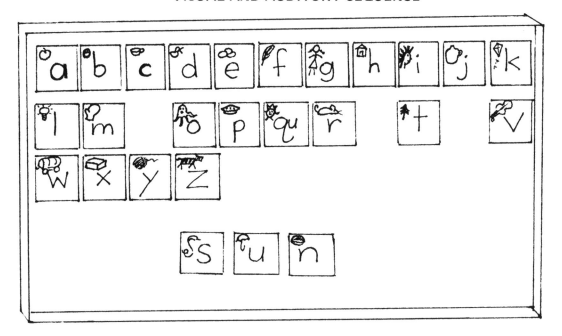

Learning letter sounds, blending and word families are most easily and accurately accomplished where the sound clue is a part of each letter card and if the letter cards are manipulative.

| | | | |
|---|---|---|---|
| Materials: | non-magnetic metal tray<br>green chalkboard paint<br>magnetic strips<br>letter set |     | |

**Assembly:** Paint metal tray with green chalkboard paint. Add an associative picture clue to the letter sound at the top left hand corner of each letter card, as illustrated. Cut small pieces of magnetic strip and glue a piece to the back of each letter card. Place on tray for easy and safe transportation and stacking. (The letters cannot fall off.)

**Uses:**

1. Begin by building word families, "Pick out the letter cards that say /at/." "Now find a letter that can be placed in front of them to make a word." Continue to build as many words as possible by changing the first letter. "Read each word you build."

2. The tray is chalkboard painted so the student can write the word he builds with chalk, right under the letter cards for kinesthetic reinforcement.

3. Teacher now sets up an initial and medial symbol (ca__) and children add endings to build words.

4. Next, practice substituting the medial sound — the vowel. "What is our word?"

5. Teacher now sounds out a word, enunciating the units and sequence carefully. "Build the word that says, 'c-a-t'."

6. Lastly, teacher holds up a picture (cat). "Build the word for this picture." Now the students should sound out the word sub-vocally. This is a more difficult level than hearing the units said distinctly by the teacher.

All this time, the associative picture clue insures accurate choice of symbol. An arrow on the tray should help reinforce left-to-right sequencing. If the children have poor speech patterns or auditory discrimination difficulties, they will need specific training in either area.

# "Alpha-Sound Program"

# 1st through 3rd

## AUDITORY:VISUAL MATCH

Many problems with the use of the phonetic analysis approach to reading and spelling are directly related to interfering factors. These factors are auditory discrimination and/or perceptual deficits — especially for short vowel sounds, blends — and hearing the units in multi-syllable words. A manipulative:associative approach is needed to increase intake accuracy, thus recall. The student must be trained in auditory recognition of sounds and sound units and must associate the sound with a particular visual unit or pattern. Auditory experiences with objects and pictures (some containing and some not containing the sound of the lesson), will tell us if he is auditorily ready and able to use a phonetic approach to reading and spelling.

Materials:    trading stamp catalog
             4½ x 11" tagboard card strip
             brass paper fastener

Procedure:  1. Look in a catalog for *pictures* having the sound of . . . (find 10).

Teach the child how to "look by vocalizing" everything he sees on a page. (Teaching how to properly scan a page is most important to the success of this project.) Vocalizing supplies the needed auditory feedback for recognition. Speech therapy may be needed for some students before they can use this approach.

Provide a KEY CARD to the sound he is seeking as a reminder (*of the sound,* not the letters.

**STEP I**

2. The class should make a list of the words for each of the correct pictures they have collected. The teacher should verify spelling to avoid negative reinforcement. Choose simple appropriate words and omit long words, where the sound unit is obscured.

The words are then to be listed by each student on his own card. Each card is headed by the associative picture clue to that sound and with all the symbols spellings that could be used. Magazine pictures are filed for sorting or other future projects.

3. Independently (homework or seat work) each student later draws a picture next to each word he has written on his card. This is essential as reinforcement and insures that he accurately rereads each word meaningfully.

4. Cards will be added as new sounds are introduced. Cards can be clipped together with a brass paper fastener or filed in a shoe box.

Every time new words or spelling lists are given they are to be added on the appropriate card(s). (Multi-syllable words might be entered on several cards.) A picture is then drawn next to these words. This step gives needed continued auditory: visual reinforcement to establish automatic response to sound/symbol patterns for spelling and reading vocabulary. Continued presence of the heading offers positive reinforcement and error-free practice.

STEP 4

38

# "Kina-Bingo" [(3)]

# All Levels

## KINESTHETIC REINFORCEMENT

"Kina-Bingo" is a term designated by the authors for their kinesthetic use of the conventional game, Bingo. Many activities or games used for lesson reinforcement are trial and error experience which offer minimal involvement. "Kina-Bingo" requires the student to look and listen, then find and trace the symbol being studied: thus, it provides a combination of auditory:visual:kinesthetic associations.

Materials: Fold sheets of paper in half and in half again. Unfold and turn the other way. Fold sheet in half and in half again. When opened, the sheet will be squared off in sixteen boxes. Letter in any sixteen lower case letters, one to a square, one one side of the sheet. Letter in upper case letters (or numbers), one to a square, on one side of the sheet. Make sets of *differently arranged* sheets to allow a small group or the whole class to play "Bingo." Enclose each in a plastic protector and supply a crayon to each child.

(3) This section is reprinted with modification, by permission of Charles C. Thomas, Publishers, *PRESCRIPTIVE TEACH-ING: Theory into Practice,* Banas and Wills, 1976.

<u>Procedure</u>: Teacher calls out, shows a picture, or shows a symbol. For example, "Find the letter that has the sound of_____," The child must find the proper one and TRACE IT. Symbols should be accompanied by an associative picture clue to its sound, so that this is *not* a trial and error activity.

<u>Uses</u>: Other sheets can be made as follows:

1) Letters (need upper and lower case set)
    a) Find the letter that makes the sound of ___ . (show picture or say)
    b) Find the upper case letter to match this letter (show).
    c) Find the lower case letter to match this letter (show).
    d) Find the letter next in the alphabet to this letter (show).
    e) Find the two (three) letters that make the word ___ .

2) Numbers (need numeral and number name sets)
    a) Find the number for this many balls (show picture)
    b) Find the number that comes after (before) ___ .
    c) Find the number name for (show or tell numeral).
    d) Find the number that answers this problem (show or ask an addition, subtraction, multiplication, or division problem).

3) Words (establish a category and make Bingo sets)
    a) Find the word that says ___ . (colors, animals, buildings, products, etc.)
    b) Find word families (words to rhyme with ___ ).
    c) Find common endings (plural of ___ ).
    d) Find roots and affixes (change this word to say ___ ).
    e) Find geographic terms (give by definition).
    f) Other.

# Go-Fish Vocabulary Builder

# All Levels

### AUDITORY:VISUAL MATCH

Materials:   Go-Fish Vocabulary Cards: Each set contains 52 cards, one half containing words, one half containing the picture for each word.

Suggested sets:   1) short vowel words

2) long vowel words

3) special category words (colors, animals, etc.)

4) numbers as quantity

5) other.

Procedure: 1.  Shuffle cards (in any combination of practice as desired; ex: short /a/ only or all short vowels)

2.  Put word list key in view of all players (2-4)

3.  Deal **4** cards to each player who keeps his cards in his hand facing him (as with regular card games). Place the rest face down on the table.

4.  Players try for a match of word with its picture.

a)  Ask player directly to the right, "Do you have the picture for ___ ?" or, "Do you have the word ___ ?" If he does, he must give it to the requester who shows his matched pair and places it on the table in front of him. If he does not, he is told to "Go, Fish," and chooses from the remainder of the cards in the middle of the table.

b)  Play continues around the table in this manner until one player has paired all of his cards and is the winner.

41

# Concentration

## all levels

AUDITORY:VISUAL MATCH

Materials:   Make sets of 20 paired cards. (Sets to be made depend upon the subject matter to be reinforced).
3 x 5" file cards, cut in half. On the face of each one draw, letter or paste pictures in accordance with the activity.

Procedure:   Shuffle the cards. Place them face down on the table in even rows. Play by turning over a card and saying what is on its face. Now, try to find a second card which will match to the first one turned over. If the second card turned over does match, the player keeps the pair, and play moves to the next student. If it is not a match, player turns both cards face down again in their same position on the table, and play moves to the next student. Continue until all cards are claimed. The student with the most pairs wins.

Uses: Sets may be made for each of the following, plus other purposes:
   1) Reading
      a) Match lower case and upper case symbols.
      b) Match lower case letters and a picture that represents the sound of each letter. (all phonetic levels, as taught)
      c) Match words with the picture that tells what the word says. For example: color words, number words, special category words, such as animals, houses, people, etc., propositions, and the current sight vocabulary words being learned.
      d) Words with missing vowels, matched to the needed vowel.

   2) Mathematics
      a) Match numeral with a dot pattern representing its value.
      b) Match problem with answer (any process).

   3) Other
      a) Geographic terms with picture referent (island, continent, etc.)
      b) Geographic shapes with name of location (states, continents, etc.)
      c) Grammatical terms and an example of their use.
      d) Foreign language and its English equivalent.

43

# The Letter Box
## 1st Grade - 3rd

### VISUAL AND AUDITORY SEQUENCE

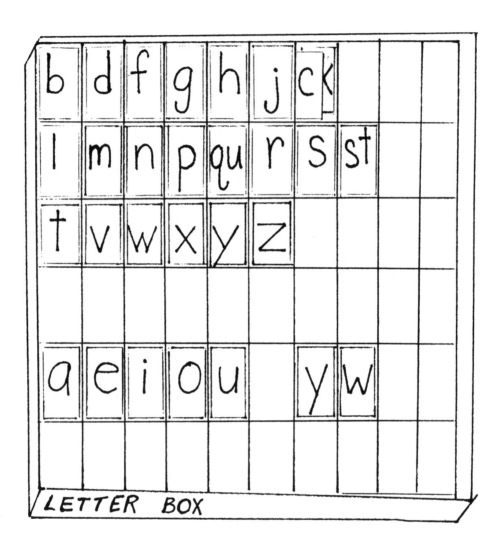

The original "letter box" was devised by Miss Edith Norrie, a Danish lady, in the late nineteen hundred's. Miss Norrie's letter box separated the letters phonetically rather than alphabetically; for example, vowels in red, voiced consonants in green, and unvoiced consonants in black. Her box contained a small mirror. As the pupil placed an appropriate letter card before him, he watched his lips as he formed its sound. A major concept of the letter box is that the child never works with isolated symbols, but always builds words (and sentences) that make sense. Thus, the letter box combines the manipulative, kinesthetic, visual, auditory and associative avenues.

Materials:    Handkerchief box 10" square

Letter Set with consonants and vowels in different colors. Note that the letter set used should represent proper spatial relationship when cards are placed side by side.

 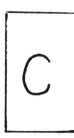   

Assembly:    Using a black marker, print the consonants in squared off segments on the bottom of the box. Note that this is done phonetically, and that the "q" is always printed with the "u". Print the vowels in red in a separate row. Remaining rows can be used for diphthongs, di-graphs, endings, etc., and added as needed. Next, place several letters in each square. Divide box with strips glued in like in egg cartons to keep the letters from shifting. Cover and stack.

Use:    Use with lessons in blending, in spelling, in syllable phonics, with English lessons, such as adding endings and building plurals, etc.

Have the children copy and/or build by choosing the letters in left-right order to form the correct total pattern in front of him. Then copy the word on his paper and replace the letters (from left to right), even if some of them are to be reused in the next word.

This may be used with oral presentation of words to be spelled, with a language box the pictures can again be used for spelling reinforcement, and with workbook lessons, such as building vowel rules, word endings, plurals, etc.

The Letter Box is being used in a spelling activity. The student says the word expressed by the picture, listens for the sounds and builds the word with the letter cards. He then turns the card over and checks and corrects his work.

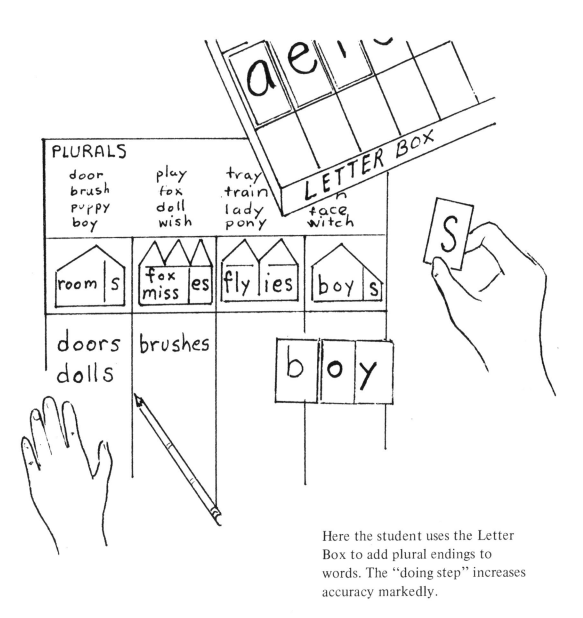

Here the student uses the Letter Box to add plural endings to words. The "doing step" increases accuracy markedly.

# "Associa-Flash Tachistoscope"
# all levels

## SIGHT RECOGNITION SPEED

To increase speed of recognition in learning a sight vocabulary, add the Associative Clue to a hand-made tachistoscope. A tachistoscope is an instrument used to increase attention and visual memory by exposing an image for a brief and measured period — usually a fraction of a second. The addition of an associative picture insures positive reinforcement responses to flashed stimuli and removes the trial and error nature of flashed programs.

Materials: Tachistoscope and Associa-Flash Strips (see illustration above) are made as needed by the teacher or student. Make a set for each reader level and use as needed to individualize practice sessions. To make the tachistoscope, tape two pieces of tagboard, 4 x 11" on the sides, leaving the top and bottom open. Cut a window. Type or print strips on tagboard, 1¼ x 11". Draw a picture clue at the far right of each word to enforce a positive response to the flashed stimuli.

Procedure: After flash exposure of each word, have the student write what he saw. Recheck his reproduction with the stimulus word. He may work with a partner and call off the words he sees.

48

# The Language Box [4]

# all levels

## READING AND LISTENING MEANINGFULLY

Because of less than accurate perceptions, some children may not have developed completely accurate concepts or visual images for words and ideas. They may need actual (real) experiences before they can attach a visual (mental) image to words that they encounter in listening or in reading context. All learning begins from our own experiences, thus training should begin with the self. Before classification can be taught, information must be available to choose from. This information is taken from spoken and written word form and held as memory. For the spoken and written word we must have a visual or experiential match.

A child learns best that which is about himself. Make a paper doll family. Have the art teacher provide cardboard models of basic family members and pets to be traced. Have the children trace a family (father, mother, himself, any siblings and others living in his household, as well as any pets). He then pastes his family on cardboard and cuts them out ready to be dressed, labeled and used in the following activities.

1. Provide a wardrobe. Again, tracing and cutting will be incorporated, but concept development and word association is involved as we guide the pupils' choice by suggesting outfits for occupations, another set for specific weather, another set for a specific activity, etc. Once made, the clothes should be labeled (on the back of each) and be stored in enveloped properly labeled as to their classification. Each envelope should also include a picture clue to its content.

It will be discovered that some items would go in more than one envelope (mother's clothes or rainy weather clothes). Make duplicates and place in both classifications.

When several types of clothing have been explored and made, they should be taken from their envelopes and randomly scattered together on the table. The children now resort to the proper envelopes using the labels as a guide. (See the illustrations on pages 50 and 51.)

---

(4) This section is reprinted with modification, by permission of Charles C. Thomas, Publishers, *PRESCRIPTIVE TEACHING: Theory into Practice,* Banas and Wills, 1976.

Mother's clothes

es

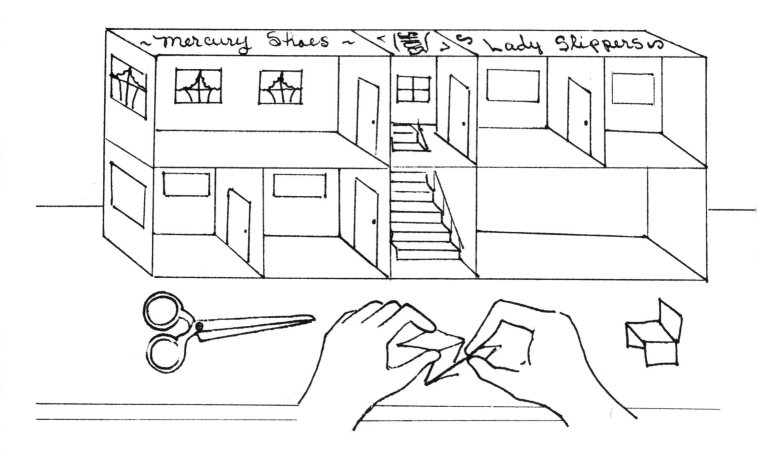

2. This activity is then extended to include the building of a home for this family. Individual, small boxes can be used to design each room with its doors and windows, and then put together in different ways to design a home and get a total perception of its part-to-whole structure.

Furniture must now be made and labeled to go with our house. To do this, the pupil develops concept and classification of appropriate furniture and furnishings for each room, as well as new sight words. Label each room and sort furniture appropriately.

52

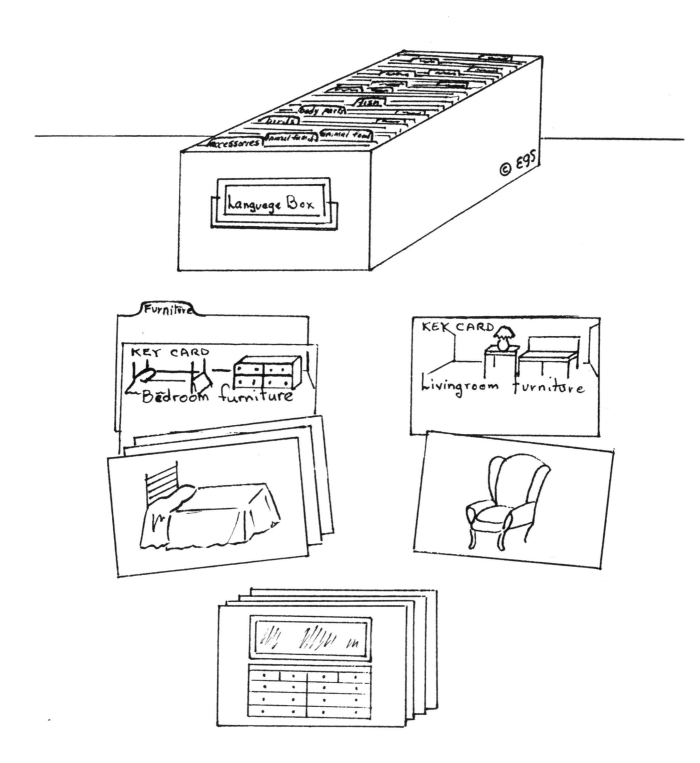

The next step is to provide file boxes (or shoe boxes) 3" x 5" x 12" and use file card dividers to set up categories. Cut pictures from books of a family, home, clothing, etc. Each should be pasted to a 3 x 5 file card for sorting and filing behind the appropriate file dividers. Working from pictures requires greater visual perception than working with manipulative and 3-dimensional material. Follow all classification and sorting steps as in Step 1 and 2.

It has been known for a long time that some people do not react to words (symbols) as representations of ideas or objects. These children cannot seem to learn by the sight word approach and do not develop a recognition vocabulary no matter how often they are flashed words or even if they use tracing techniques to learn the word form. These children may learn to use a phonetic attack, but they will be found to sound out every word, time and again, no matter how often that word appears on a given page. It is obvious that a phonetic approach which does not lead to automatic recognition of words cannot carry him to a very high level of reading achievement, and the effort it takes to decode words does not allow him energies or attention to what the words and context are saying. Associative word pictures and Kina-writing as outlined in Chapter One have helped with the development of sight words and spelling memory. However, these are slow processes, and only so many new words a day can be so introduced. Since the basic principle involved is the need to associate the word (symbol) and its referent (the real object or a visual image of the experience or object), the language box can be utilized to provide this associative experience.

1. The word that labels or expresses the content of the picture should be printed on the back of each picture card. Another set of these words is to be made on small size slips. These word slips are to be filed with the appropriate set of picture cards and used in sorting to the pictures. The picture card is then turned over to insure accuracy in associating the correct picture and word.

2. Experience stories should then be made to accompany each set of picture cards. Use the picture/words over and over so there is sufficient reinforcement in context. Do not try this reading activity until the children have enough accurate practice sorting the word and picture cards to each other.

# CATEGORIES FOR LANGUAGE BOX

accessories (personal)

animal families

animal food

animal parts

animal products

birds

body parts

building parts

buildings

clothing

colors

emotions

fish

food

furniture

insects

natural phenomena

occupations

people

places

plants

plant products

reptiles

rooms

sports

toys and games

vehicles

# Associative Stories

## Reading with a Purpose

Some children cannot seem to learn words presented in any of the known techniques. These children may be showing a lack of identification with the significance of words. If they do not identify with or have a frame-of-reference for words for reading, putting the "self" into the content may give the children an involvement, an interest, and an awareness of the value of words, so that they are motivated to begin reading.

Materials: photographs of the child, members of his family, his pets, his house, etc.
  plain (unlined) white bond paper
  typewriter

Procedures: Begin with a photograph of the child. Help him to verbalize about himself from the picture and write "his story" with him. The teacher *must* use words which the child *is in need of learning,* and must *control the vocabulary,* so that a *few basic words* are *repeated over and over again in each story and from story to story.* A careful control of this vocabulary is the key to experience story success as sight vocabulary develops. For example:

This is Larry.

He is a boy.

He has brown hair.

He has brown eyes.

His birthday is July 8.

He is eight years old.

Experience stories are of little value if the words introduced are not those to be used in other contexts at this level by this child, or if the words are not repeated often enough to establish familiarity.

Type his story (on primer typewriter if possible) on unlined bond with double spaces between lines. Attach his picture. Place in a notebook.

Read and reread his story with him that day and each day following as his "Family Album" grows page by page into a book. This approach was developed by Mrs. Frances McGlannan at the McGlannan School, Miami, Florida.

Each day add another page to "his" book with a photograph to motivate interest and create a meaningful story. Cover his home, each member of his family, his pets, his friends, his hobbies, etc. Be sure to continue the vocabulary from one page to the next. Guide the introduction and repetition of words, yet the story content will be child's own environment. Develop insights, concepts, relationships, as well as vocabulary and reading skills.

Variation: Words and punctuation should be printed one each on 2" x 2" index card strips to be used in building new sentences related to, or in isolation of, the Associative Story. A key to the word in the form of a picture should be placed on the back, so that these become flash cards which can be used independently with assurance of positive successful reinforcement. Child may enjoy building rebus picture sentences with the picture side and slowly make the change to the word side. Punctuation is learned and reinforced in this way, too, as he must add the card containing the correct end punctuation and insert comma cards where needed.

# More Meaning to
# Reading, Writing and Spelling

Punctuation, capitalization and word endings are too often taught as isolated skills. In reality, these skills help us read and write meaningfully. Punctuation, capitalization and altered word endings provide for changes in the meaning of the words we read. So it is important that punctuation and changes in word endings be taught in context (in sentences).

It has been found that the Associative Approach through meaningful stories and meaningful picture clues helps recall of these arbitrary, but important symbols. Associative clues can be in the form of stories or in the form of picture associations. Whichever form is used in establishing meaning for the symbols, the use of a static visual reminder must follow the initial lesson. The sample worksheets which follow all provide, in some way, a static visual clue, which hopefully will trigger recall of the story or picture association which was the basis of the introductory lesson. Continued use of static visual clues until the concepts and symbols are well learned *is a must*. The change from the use of the picture or story clue to the use of the symbol by itself must be gradual, so that transfer is smoothly effected. These worksheets are but examples of how to use the associative story approach to teach the many arbitrary rules of our language.

Mike said Hello.

1. Put a stick figure person over the boy who is speaking to you in the sentence above.

2. Lasso the words he said to you. (like in the cartoons)

3. Substitute quotation marks " " for the lasso in the sentence below.

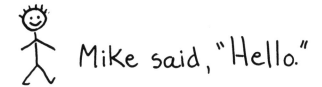

Mike said Hello.

4. Put, in red, a comma just before the word he said in the above sentence.

5. In each of the following sentences, draw a stick figure picture of the speaker and lasso the words he says. Then rewrite each sentence, substituting quotation marks for the lasso and placing a comma before the spoken words.

a. Bob called out How are you.

   _____

b. My name is Sam I said.

   _____

c. John asked where are you going?

   _____

d. Mary cried I hurt my toe.

   _____

**COMMAS**     (,)             Name_____

                                                Date_____

---

1. List of foods

   milk   chocolate   peanut   butter   apple   pie   ice   cream

2. Make two lists from the words above of food you might eat. There will be eight in list A, but only 4 foods in list B.*

                     **A.**                                         **B.**

   _____                 _____

   _____                 _____

   _____                 _____

   _____                 _____

   _____

   _____

   _____

   _____

3. Show how to list the foods in column A. above by placing them in the following sentence and placing a comma (,) between each item.

   I wish to order _____ , _____ , _____ , _____ , _____ , _____ , _____ , _____ .

4. Now order from list B. Remember to place a comma between each item.

   I wish to order _____ , _____ , _____ , _____ .

5. Read list A. to the class. Can they guess how many items you plan to order? Now read list B.

I. Instructions:

A. Please come home 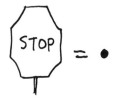 = •

This is a STATEMENT. Once said you can stop. It requires no answer nor action.

B. Fire    Come home quickly

This is an EXCLAMATION. It requires immediate attention and action.

C. Will you come home

This is a QUESTION. It requires an answer from someone.

II. Assignment:
Place the proper sign after each of the following sentences.
(Assign appropriate sentences, as desired.)

**PLURALS**

Name_____

Date_____

Make plurals of the following words after putting them in the correct column below.

| door | play | fix | tray |
|------|------|-----|------|
| brush | party | bunch | story |
| puppy | fox | lady | school |
| turkey | miss | toy | wish |
| witch | doll | pony | train |

**TEACHER'S INSTRUCTIONS**

The teacher should tell the following story as she builds the illustration from the heading on the board. After an initial presentation and practice, this worksheet is presented to each student as a static visual clue to the story which illustrates the rules for adding plural endings. If the more perceptually impaired or slower learning children cannot follow the concept of matching each word to the proper column and thus changing the ending according to that specific rule, then they should cut out each of the four headings and use them as manipulative Key Cards. The manipulative, sorting step can help them "see" where the purely visual activity does not.

Story: "The family that lives in our first house is a simple family (an ordinary word) who lives in only one room. They want to make their house bigger and have more room, so they add a storage space (S). (Draw as you talk.) Their next door neighbor, Miss Fox, has a fancy house with a storage space (ES). Her neighbor, Mr. Fry, wants to be fancy, so he adds a whole extra space (ES). She decides to make her place larger by adding it into a sliding panel alters his house by taking out one wall (y) and changing it into a sliding panel with a push button opener (i), then adds his extra space (ES). The boy next door to him gets all excited and says, 'Wow, our name ends in y, so can we have a sliding panel, too?' But his Dad says, 'No, we cannot, because if we did that, we would have three vowels in a row (oie), and that is not allowed on our block. We must add only a simple storage space (S).'"

62

Add -ed and - ing to the words below after putting them in the correct column.

| ten | bush | belt | hope | back |
| wait | pin | ship | pat | pa pain |
| pine | camp | time | live | lean |

| — ed | — ed | — ed | — ed |
|---|---|---|---|
| pet_t_ed | steamed | bŭshed | baked |

**TEACHER'S INSTRUCTIONS**

The teacher first tells the following story, using a manipulative word and word ending card set, then passes out these worksheets which provide a static visual clue to recall of the rule learned.

Story: "Remember our vowel friends, a, e, i, o, u? Remember that when they walk alone they say their short sound (say each). When we want to show something happened in the past, we often add "-ed" to a word. Watch what happens if we add -ed to our short vowel wor. (Move an -ed letter card to join a short vowel word card) . . . see that our vowel sound changes because the "magic e" has joined the end of the line. We don't want to change the sound of our vowel, as it would change the meaning of our word (pet = Pete), so what can we do? We can put an extra letter into our word to keep the "magic e" from changing our vowel sound; let's make that letter the same as the last letter in our word. Now we can add -ed. Notice that our next word already has a long vowel sound (steam), so let's go right ahead and add -ed. Now look at our next word, bush; it already has two consonants (sh) to separate the vowels, so that it can't hurt to add the -ed right away. Our last word already has an "e" on the end. It would be wasteful to add another "e", so let's just add the "d"."

63

©egs

Name_____

Date_____

Add - ed and -ing to the following words after putting them in the correct column below.

| pine | hop | dome | scrap |
|------|------|------|--------|
| pin | hope | wait | scrape |
| dance | ship | fin | pain |
| scrub | drag | fire | live |

| – ed | – d | – ing | – ing |
|------|------|--------|--------|
| stop **P** ed | file__d | stop **P** ing | fil**✗** ing |

**TEACHER'S INSTRUCTIONS**

This worksheet is a follow-up to learning to add -ed. Remind the students about the need to put in an extra consonant to keep the "magic e" from changing our short vowel word meaning. Then show the class that this situation is also true when adding -ing (i acts like the magic e). Remind them to add -d only if our word ends in -e, but point out the need to remove the -e if adding -ing, so we don't put the two vowels together.

64

© egs

ADDING ENDINGS    —    ING

Name_____

Date_____

Add — ing to each word below after putting it in the correct column. Use each — ing word in a sentence in the space below.

| pine | come | face | climb | dive |
|------|------|------|-------|------|
| wait | play | race | ride | drive |
| steam | pain | jump | see | bait |

— ing
pine = pining

— ing
rain = raining

— ing
pump = pumping

Sentence:

TEACHER'S INSTRUCTIONS

More -ing uses. Remind the class that adding -ing to the words ending in -e requires removing the -e first. Show them that the middle word already has a long vowel sound, so, like the adding -ed, we can go right ahead and add -ing with no change of sound. In the last case, we see that we have two consonants at the end, so we can add -ing again without changing the vowel sound.

## CAPITAL LETTERS

Worksheet A. on capital letters is basically self-explanatory, but like any good teaching experience, needs a lesson preceding the use of the worksheet.

Teach the children that, when they give a particular name to a place or person, they then must use capital letters. Note that the worksheet gives the common name (noun) in each section. Ask the children to use the particular (proper) name (noun) for each and fill in on the blanks provided.

Worksheet B. gives an additional visual experience in turning common names for persons or places into proper names for the same person or place. Children must now fill in first the uncapitalized, common name; then fill in their choice of a particular (proper) name using capital letters for each.

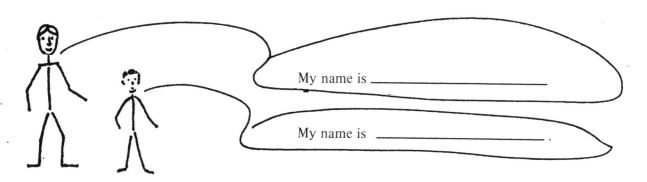

1. Fill in a name for each person above. Since it is their proper name, it should begin with a capital letter. Give them a first, middle and last name.

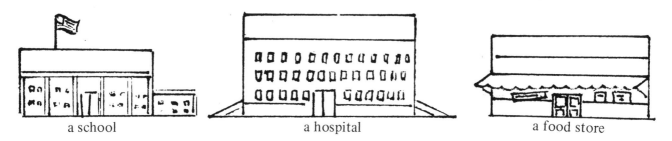

a school                a hospital                a food store

2. Each of the buildings above have a particular (proper) name. Think of the name of your school, hospital and food store and put the names on the space provided. Be sure to begin each word of the signs with a capital letter.

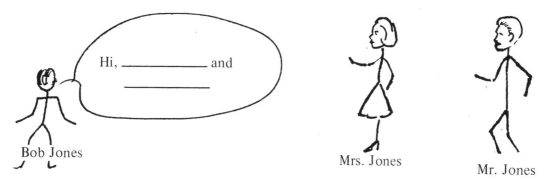

Hi, _____ and _____

Bob Jones                Mrs. Jones                Mr. Jones

3. Mrs. Jones is Bobby's mother. Mother is another name for Mrs. Jones. Place the word, Mother, on one line, and be sure to start it with a capital letter. Mr. Jones is his father. Put his name on the other line.

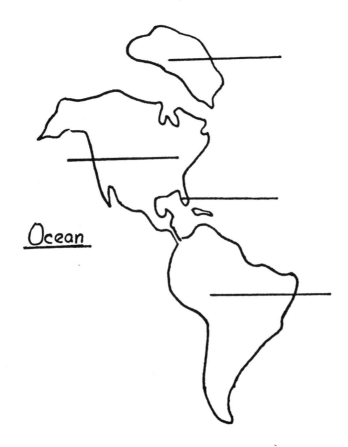

Ocean

4. This is a map. Each place has its own proper name. Each name must therefore begin with a capital letter. Find out the name of each place and put it on the proper line.

| Report Card |
| --- |
| reading |
| spelling |
| english |
| geography |
| u.s. history |
| spanish |

5. When we study a subject in school that is named after a country, we must begin that word with a capital letter. Find and capitalize each subject in the above report card whose name comes from the name of a country.

Date _____

Fill in the blanks in each sentence with the proper word.

| Common Nouns | Proper Nouns |
|---|---|

I see the _____ .                                      I see _____ .

I see the _____ .                                      I see _____ .

I go to _____ .                                    I go to the _____ .

I shop at the _____ .                              I shop at _____ .

I live on that _____ .                              I live on _____ .

I like the _____ .                                    I like the _____ .

He is captain of the _____ .                    He is captain of the _____ .

I have fun at the _____ .                          I have fun at _____ .

69

# Chapter III

# MAKING MATH MEANINGFUL

**Math Defined:**

Math is a visual-spatial ability. This refers to the ability to see and to visualize (get a mental image of) space. Space refers to distance, volume, quantity and time or duration of time. Mathematics is used, among other things, to measure the size of material objects and to discover their properties (as in its use with mechanics). Arithmetic, a division of mathematics, is the science of numbers or the ability to do computation with the fundamental operations of addition, subtraction, multiplication, and division.

**Boys vs. Girls:**

Many people feel that boys are better at math than are girls. To an extent, this may be true, as it has been noted that boys more often possess better visual-spatial tial ability. About half of all boys and about one-fourth of all girls seem to be born with this special ability. It is also true that culturally and environmentally we may be offering boys, more than girls, the early experiences that help them develop good visual-spatial skills.

**Body Awareness:**

The development of inherent visual-spatial skills begins with early exploration by the infant of his world. He explores it physically with his limbs and his whole body, and his physical experiences teach him about distance, size, shape, position, volume, and quantity. Direct experiences take time and are often limited, but cannot be skipped in his developmental years.

71

Playground activity helps children experience distance, duration, direction, and size and space relationships.

Arts, crafts, construction toys and other materials provide experiences in size, space, position and spatial relationship.

Music and rhythmic activities such as jump rope, dancing, and some sports develop duration of time awareness.

Experiences with measuring devices and containers at home or at school help children learn size, quantity and volume.

73

Direct experiences are of recognized value and are, thus, incorporated into many math programs, where the use of rectangular blocks, for example, help children learn size, space and position relationships.

**Vision**: Vision soon becomes the major avenue through which we perceive space. At first, direct contact is used to measure size and distance dimensions. Our eyes are also transmitting messages about size distance to the brain through muscle movement. Soon we learn to use and rely on the visual messages alone. We learn that the further away an object is, the smaller it appears to us; we note that if distant objects overlap, the overlapping object is closer. The position of the eyeballs tells us distance, as our eyes turn inward as an object comes closer to us. Thus, good visual skills are essential to the development of visual-spatial ability for math.

Some of the specific visual skills which would affect our awareness and success in relating to our environment are listed and defined below. For a developmental approach to the appraisal of visual skills in relation to learning, see Banas and Wills, *Identifying Early Learning Ga ps,* Humanics Limited, Atlanta, Georgia, 1975.

**Accommodation**: The shifting of focus from one distance to another distance. To do this, the muscles contract and relax. It is like adjusting the lens of a camera to bring distant objects into clear focus, but the whole process for us is automatic and rapid. With many experiences the tension experienced by the muscles supplies signals to our brain which tell us the distance of an object.

**Convergence**: The focusing of both eyes on an object requires a turning inward of each eye until the object is brought into view as a single image. This is similar to the converging lines which the artist uses to show distance. Again, the muscles which control the movement of the eyeballs in their sockets signal our brain which learns to associate movement and distance.

**Pursuit Ability**: The ability to follow a moving object with the eye needs to be accurate or the child may skip symbols, lose his place, be slow in finding his place, and may not be able to follow the teacher's explanation as she illustrates a lesson.

**Fixation**: The ability to fix one's vision at a specific place accurately and rapidly is needed in order to follow visual referents, to read, to work with math problems, and to keep his place. Many children with difficulty fixating are found to become tense and even hyperactive because of the stress in focusing their vision on the essential part of the stimuli.

Visual skills training as provided by professionals specializing in visual skills therapy can do a great deal to increase visual efficiency, thus academic endeavors. **Directionality:** Directionality, or the spatial relations of an object in relation to self or other objects, is very crucial in reading, writing and math. At first the child locates objects in relation to himself. Later he learns about objects in relation to each other. In exploring and viewing the environment choice in viewing from left-to-right or up or down, etc. is of no importance. However, the moment the child reaches the symbol stage, left-to-right viewing is essential. It is the spatial relationship of symbols that gives them specific (and changing) meaning. For example, the sound of the symbol "A" changes with its relationship to other symbols in the series. Thus, cat becomes coat becomes car becomes caught becomes warm. We read numbers and visualize their value correctly only if we read them from left-to-right: 21 or 12? Just as the child grasps the need to work from left-to-right in order to "read" symbols, he is told that he must work from right-to-left to compute in math. Place value is a math term given to the (spatial) position of the symbol which determines its value (2 or 20 or 200?). Some children cannot make this shift from reading left-to-right, then working right-to-left for math. Many children have such poorly developed directionality awareness that they work inconsistently and unpredictably from day to day.

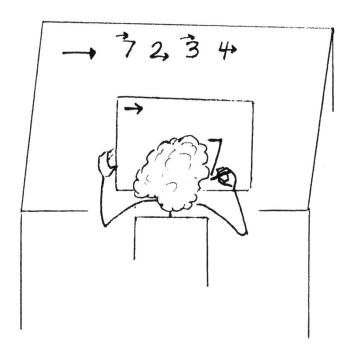

For some children, an arrow placed at the top of their work table or paper can be a major aid in directional accuracy in forming symbols.

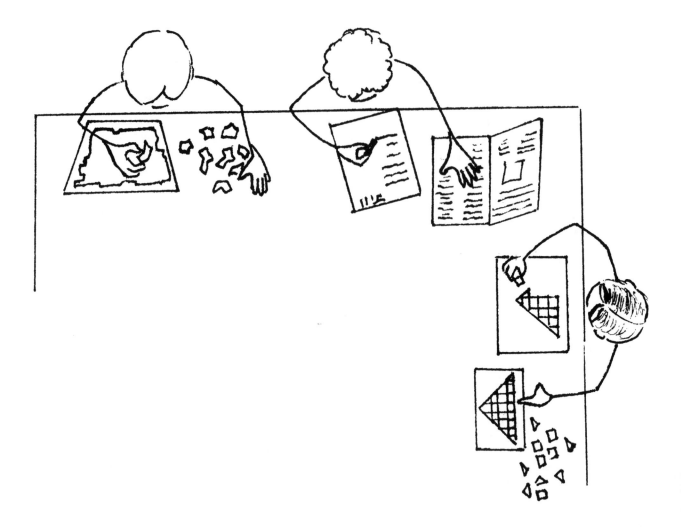

All work should be presented at the left (or at the top) of his work paper, so that viewing is automatically left-to-right. Consistency in this positioning of work or play materials throughout the day can be important in establishing automatic and lasting left-to-right viewing habits.

**Laterality**: Directionality is the external awareness of position in space of objects while *laterality is the internal awareness of the two-sidedness of the body.* The development of laterality can be noted in attempts to balance. Laterality helps us develop an awareness of the horizontal dimension of space, and leads to awareness of leftness and rightness outside our body. Gravity and the pull it exerts on us in falling forward and backward and in holding objects down or allowing them to move upward helps us learn about other directions of space.

Since laterality is reflected in balance, the use of balance boards and walking rails has been incorporated into playground experiences.

Gravity can be experienced readily in diving and jumping. It has led to the use of swimming and gymnastics as well as the use of a trampoline in developing spatial skills.

**Figure:Ground Perception**: Spatial awareness begins with body awareness and the three-dimensional world. It must, however, be projected to vision and the recognition of position with two-dimensional space and with linear and abstract symbols. Some children cannot make this transition from the three-dimensional world to its linear representations and are said to have "a visual perceptual deficit or lag."

One of the most interfering factors is a lag in development of figure:ground perception. This is the ability to focus on and note pertinent details from among a background of data. The child who cannot find what is under his nose, or the student who can handle a problem when it is in isolation as on a flash card, but can not handle it when it is on a full page of problems, may be experiencing difficulty with figure:ground perception. A lag in figure:ground perception will ead the child to make the so-called "careless" errors in math, to skip whole problems, to lose his place, and to miss the signs and fail to shift from addition to subtraction, for example.

The boy has a

big red kite. It

is taller than he

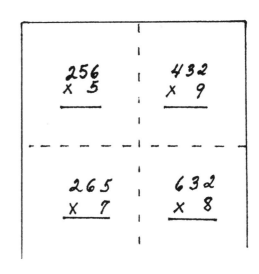

256
x 5

432
x 9

265
x 7

632
x 8

When we first

came to visit Miss

Patty, I tho... as

very odd to se

Sight Saver Books

Jerry went
to the store
to buy some
milk. He

Underlining, color coding, large spacing around each problem, uncluttered pages, and large bold forms can be big aids to reducing errors. Dittos should be very carefully used as the light purple ink is very difficult for children with perceptual lags. Lined paper can be more a detriment than an aid as it may cause the student to write too small, it does not help him space his problems far enough apart, and its very lines form a visual distraction. Plain newsprint is best utilized. If unlined paper is folded in half and in half again, turned the other way and folded in half and in half again, when opened it will provide sixteen boxes in which to place problems. This has proven an effective method of reducing errors for children with perceptual or motor lags.

## TRANSFERRING TO SYMBOLS

**Manipulative Materials** are an important aid as they intensify the stimuli and help bridge the transfer from the three-dimensional world to the linear world. By placing a symbol on the object, an association is made. When the object is removed, the visual image of it remains whenever the child sees the symbol.

All manipulative materials must accurately represent the size, position, space, and quantity relationship being learned. The appropriate symbol should *always* accompany the manipulative material, so that when the manipulative aid is removed, and the child works entirely with symbols, hopefully he will visualize the meaning and value of the symbol because of its previous consistent association with its referent.

**Associative Picture Clue:** For many children, manipulative experiences are not sufficient for meaningful recall of the symbol, and a very highly associative clue is needed. This can be provided in the form of "pictograms," or a picture clue to the meaning of the symbol as illustrated above.

The "Associa-Math" program takes the student through a step-by-step process of teaching and reinforcing addition, subtraction, multiplication and division. It incorporates the use of manipulative materials, color coding, associative pictograms, and takes into consideration the need for varying lengths of reinforcement periods for individual students.

If there is a basic or underlying developmental lag or deficit in visual-spatial skills, clinical remediation may be needed in addition to the math program offered herewith. For an in-depth, developmental program of visual and motor skills, read Banas and Wills, *Prescriptive Teaching: Theory into Practice,* Charles C. Thomas, Publishers, Springfield, Ill. 1976.

# Associa-Math Program

# Phase No. 1
# Addition and Subtraction

**Basic Principles:**

Use number bars as illustrated below. The number bars develop awareness of the inverse relationship of addition problems. The presence of the symbol helps the student visualize and transfer from the manipulative:meaningful learning experience to the linear:symbol activity.

Example:

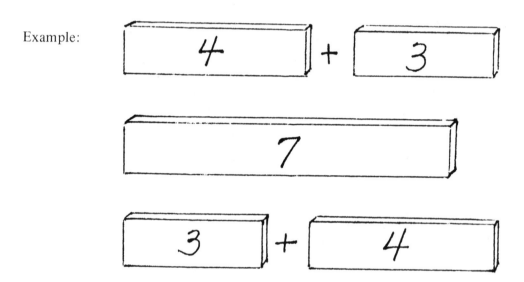

Associative keys and color coded, controlled flash card sets are needed for a step-by-step program of concept development to make math symbols more meaningful and to increase recall of number facts.

"Associa-math," a term devised by the authors, employs meaningful associations between the action and its symbol referent (addition = +) or between a quantity ($\ominus$ = 1) and its symbol referent. Children with perceptual deficits or lags may have difficulty with recall because of confused images in the initial learning stages. Trial and error or test practice situations are to be avoided at all costs. The perceptually impaired child will not be able to sort which image (the correct or incorrect) was the desired one.

For many children a difficulty in working with subtraction may be a difficulty in shifting from one type of stimulus:response to another. For others, it may be that they do not "see" the relationship between the addition sets and subtraction facts.

The following approach provides error-free practice for positive reinforcement while gaining speed and accuracy.

FOOTNOTE: See *Math Magic,* Selma Kahn, Humanics Limited, 1975, for other manipulative materials.

Use the number bars and begin with the 5 set. Build all the addition combinations which make 5. This helps reinforce accurate visualizations and recall of addition facts while teaching subtraction.

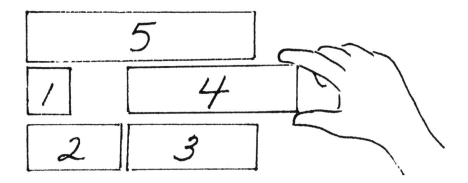

Establish the concept that subtraction is thinking of the missing number or the other number in the addition set. Ask him to physically "Take away 4," by having the pupil move the strip to show he "sees" which number in a set to take away. "What is left when we take 4 away from a 5 set?" He should "see" that the remaining number bar is the answer. This process gives complete meaning to the term, "take away." Later introduce the terms, "subtract" and "minus" as meaning the same thing as "take away."

3. Use the same material and place only ones bars under the 5 bar. Introduce and reinforce the idea that subtraction works only when a smaller or equal *quantity* (represented by one or more symbols) is taken from a larger or equal *quantity*.

Let the students discover that the *quantity* represented by 5 ones can be also represented as:

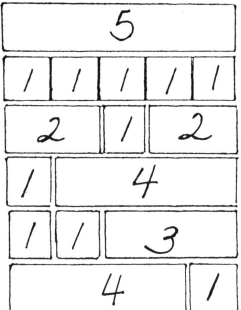

Materials:

Make "associa-key" and "associa-flash" card sets on 3"x5" file cards with color coding as indicated. These provide individual, independent, error-free practice so each pupil can work at his own pace and level. Use as instructed on pages 85 and 86.

**KEY CARDS**                    (orange) **FIVES:**                    **FLASH CARDS**

5:  4 + 1 =
    3 + 2 =

$$\begin{array}{ccccc} 5 & 5 & 5 & 5 & 5 \\ -\underline{1} & \underline{2} & \underline{3} & \underline{4} & \underline{5} \end{array} \qquad \begin{array}{ccc} 4 & 3 & 2 \\ +\underline{1} & +\underline{2} & +\underline{3} \end{array}$$

(green) **SIXES:**

6:  5 + 1 =
    4 + 2 =
    3 + 3 =

$$\begin{array}{ccccc} 6 & 6 & 6 & 6 & 6 \\ -\underline{1} & \underline{2} & \underline{3} & \underline{4} & \underline{5} \end{array} \qquad \begin{array}{cccc} 5 & 4 & 3 & 2 \\ +\underline{1} & \underline{2} & \underline{3} & \underline{4} \end{array}$$

(white) **SEVENS:**

7:  6 + 1 =
    5 + 2 =
    4 + 3 =

$$\begin{array}{cccccc} 7 & 7 & 7 & 7 & 7 & 7 \\ -\underline{1} & \underline{2} & \underline{3} & \underline{4} & \underline{5} & \underline{6} \end{array} \qquad \begin{array}{ccccc} 6 & 5 & 4 & 3 & 2 \\ +\underline{1} & \underline{2} & \underline{3} & \underline{4} & \underline{5} \end{array}$$

(blue) **EIGHTS:**

8:  7 + 1 =
    6 + 2 =
    5 + 3 =
    4 + 4 =

$$\begin{array}{ccccccc} 8 & 8 & 8 & 8 & 8 & 8 & 8 \\ -\underline{1} & \underline{2} & \underline{3} & \underline{4} & \underline{5} & \underline{6} & \underline{7} \end{array} \qquad \begin{array}{cccccc} 7 & 6 & 5 & 4 & 3 & 2 \\ +\underline{1} & \underline{2} & \underline{3} & \underline{4} & \underline{5} & \underline{6} \end{array}$$

(yellow) **NINES:**

9:  8 + 1 =
    7 + 2 =
    6 + 3 =
    5 + 4 =

$$\begin{array}{ccccccc} 9 & 9 & 9 & 9 & 9 & 9 & 9 \\ -\underline{1} & \underline{2} & \underline{3} & \underline{4} & \underline{5} & \underline{6} & \underline{7} \end{array} \qquad \begin{array}{ccccc} 8 & 7 & 6 & 5 & 4 \\ +\underline{1} & \underline{2} & \underline{3} & \underline{4} & \underline{5} \end{array} \text{etc.}$$

(orange) **TENS:**

10:  9 + 1 =
     8 + 2 =
     7 + 3 =
     6 + 4 =
     5 + 5 =

$$\begin{array}{cccccccc} 10 & 10 & 10 & 10 & 10 & 10 & 10 & 10 \\ -\underline{1} & \underline{2} & \underline{3} & \underline{4} & \underline{5} & \underline{6} & \underline{7} & \underline{8} \end{array} \qquad \begin{array}{c} 9 \\ +\underline{1} \end{array} \text{etc.}$$

**Put proper sign on all flash cards.**

Daily Procedure:

      Give each child his own set of flash cards and key cards. Be sure that he can see the relationship between the key card and the bars used in the first step (pg. 83). If he cannot make the shift easily, put a box around the numbers on his key card to emulate the bars as illustrated below.

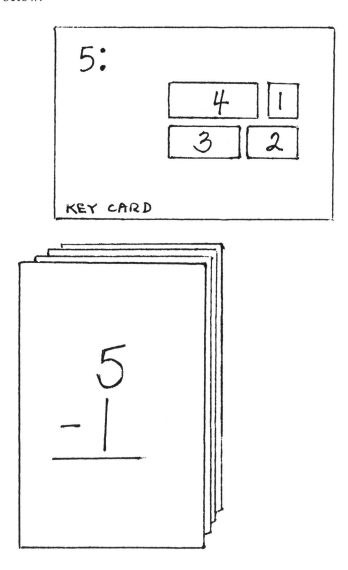

      Teach him to place a finger on the key card over the number to be taken away. This helps him "see" the number taken away. Later, he can do this just by looking.

      Introduce combinations of 5 and of 6. Color coding is a *must* because of its value in helping students shift from one set to another.

      Instruct the child to, "Take out your key cards and place them at the top of your desk (in sequential order). Shuffle both sets of flash cards together. Place the shuffled flash cards *at the left* of your work paper. (Always work left to right.) Write your problem and answer (always referring to your key) on your paper." See illustration on page 86.

It is preferable to use unlined paper folded to form boxes into which to place each problem. This is an aid to space use and important to all children with perceptual or motor lags.

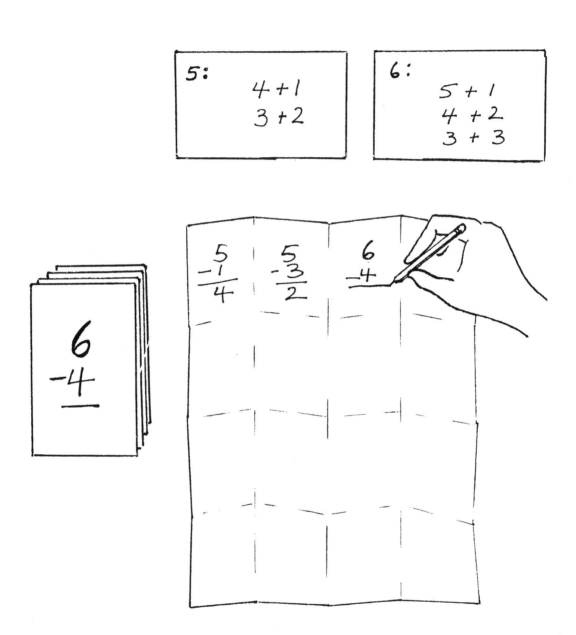

Practice with 5's and 6's ONCE EACH DAY for the entire week. The second week, *add* the 7 set. The class will still work with 5's and 6's for another week while 7's are added and shuffled in with them. The third week remove 5's for those children who know them without looking at the key, and add 8's. Next week remove 6's and add 9's. Then remove 7's and add 10's. Following this routine, addition and removal would depend upon the speed of the child in gaining recall.

Most children will stop looking at the keys, except to check their work, as soon as they are able. Some children may remain dependent because it is easier than learning their number facts. For these children, remove their key cards to a table across a room. Now he must write the problem, get up, go to the key, hold the an swer in his head, and return to put it on his paper.

# Associa-Math Program

# Phase No. 2

## ADDITION AND SUBTRACTION

Materials:    Associa-Flash Card Set B.
                Number Lines

Procedure:

Each child should have his own set of flash cards as illustrated on pages 89 through 97. The order of introduction must be followed as outlined. Each key card offers an association to aid recall.

By taking the easy to visualize combinations (1's, 2's, 5's, number by self, and 9's) and reinforcing the inverse process of addition, the remaining number sets leave little to be memorized.

Instruct child to, "Remove key card(s) and place them in front of you on the desk. Shuffle your flash card sets together; place them at the left of your work paper; write each problem, and answer, referring to the key to be sure you get the right answer." Using the key, he answers his problems in error-free practice for positive reinforcement.

Reshuffling the cards again and again, the children have unlimited practice without the need for a Workbook. They can work on their specific area(s) of need with as much reinforcement as needed by each pupil.

Variation:

    1. At all levels, use the "long range keys" technique to develop recall, where necessary.

    2. Math concentration cards can be made by the class. These should also be used with the Key Cards to insure reinforcement of correct responses.

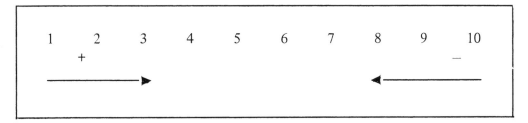

Review speed of recognition of "one more" and "one less" with number line. First practice orally, and then use flash cards. Have child touch the number and move his finger in the necessary direction (+ or −) to reinforce kinesthetically. Addition moves upward (to the right) in number value and subtraction moves downward (to the left) in number value.

Associa-flash cards: (pink cards)

| 1 | 2 | 3 | 4 | 5 | 6 | 7 | 8 | 9 |
|---|---|---|---|---|---|---|---|---|
| +1 | 1 | 1 | 1 | 1 | 1 | 1 | 1 | 1 |

| 2 | 3 | 4 | 5 | 6 | 7 | 8 | 9 |
|---|---|---|---|---|---|---|---|
| −1 | 1 | 1 | 1 | 1 | 1 | 1 | 1 |

Adding by ending: make as desired

| 20 | 30 | etc. | 12 | 13 | etc. | 22 | 32 | etc. | 25 | 31 | etc. |
|---|---|---|---|---|---|---|---|---|---|---|---|
| +1 | +1 | | +1 | +1 | | +1 | +1 | | +11 | +16 | |

Specific attention to change in tens column is needed, but do not teach as regrouping at this point. Work for automatic response of one more and one less.

| 19 | 29 | 39 | 49 | 59 | 69 | 79 | 89 | 99 |
|---|---|---|---|---|---|---|---|---|
| +1 | 1 | 1 | 1 | 1 | 1 | 1 | 1 | 1 |

| 20 | 30 | 40 | 50 | 60 | 70 | 80 | 90 | 100 |
|---|---|---|---|---|---|---|---|---|
| +1 | 1 | 1 | 1 | 1 | 1 | 1 | 1 | 1 |

NOTE: All cards must carry the proper sign.

Odd numbers — red ink
Even numbers — black ink

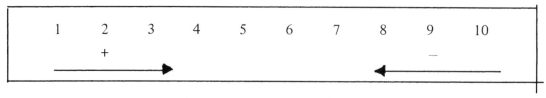

Use the same process as with $\pm$ 1, but the color coding will help the child see to move "two more" or "two less" on the number line. <u>Discourage counting</u> and encourage visualizing the skipping of one number in moving "two more" or "two less."

Associa-flash cards: (blue cards)

| 2 | 3 | 4 | 5 | 6 | 7 | 8 | 9 |
|----|----|----|----|----|----|----|----|
| +2 | +2 | +2 | +2 | +2 | +2 | +2 | +2 |

| 3 | 4 | 5 | 6 | 7 | 8 | 9 |
|----|----|----|----|----|----|----|
| −2 | −2 | −2 | −2 | −2 | −2 | −2 |

Adding by endings:

| 12 | 13 | 14 | 15 | 16 | 17 | | 62 | | 25 |
|----|----|----|----|----|----|----|----|----|----|
| +2 | +2 | +2 | +2 | +2 | +2 | | −2 | | −22 |

Continue as desired, but use no regrouping at this point.

Subtracting by endings:

| 12 | 13 | 14 | 15 | 16 | 17 | 18 | 19 |
|----|----|----|----|----|----|----|----|
| −2 | −2 | −2 | −2 | −2 | −2 | −2 | −2 |

Continue as desired.

90

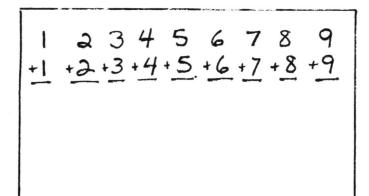

(put answers <u>in pencil</u>)

$$\begin{array}{cccccccccc} 1 & 2 & 3 & 4 & 5 & 6 & 7 & 8 & 9 \\ +1 & +2 & +3 & +4 & +5 & +6 & +7 & +8 & +9 \\ \hline \end{array}$$

Associa-flash cards: (blue cards)

$$\begin{array}{cccccccccc} 1 & 2 & 3 & 4 & 5 & 6 & 7 & 8 & 9 \\ +\,1 & +\,2 & +\,3 & +\,4 & +\,5 & +\,6 & +\,7 & +\,8 & +\,9 \\ \hline \end{array}$$

$$\begin{array}{ccccc} 10 & 12 & 14 & 16 & 18 \\ -5 & -6 & -7 & -8 & -9 \\ \hline \end{array}$$

$$\begin{array}{cccccccccc} 10 & 20 & 30 & 40 & 50 & 60 & 70 & 80 & 90 & 100 \\ +\,10 & +\,20 & +\,30 & +\,40 & +\,50 & +\,60 & +\,70 & +\,80 & +\,90 & +\,100 \\ \hline \end{array}$$

Doubles must be memorized; there is no trick or easier way to learn them. At first, the key card should contain all the answers, IN PENCIL. As the individual child learns each double, he can erase that answer. Practice until no answers remain on the key card.

Use the doubles key card. Introduce the idea that recall of combinations just one less than doubles can be aided by first thinking of the double of the larger number, then think "one less." For example:

Associa-Flash Cards: (pink cards)

| 1 | 2 | 3 | 4 | 5 | 6 | 7 | 8 |
|---|---|---|---|---|---|---|---|
| + 2 | + 3 | + 4 | + 5 | + 6 | + 7 | + 8 | + 9 |

| 2 | 3 | 4 | 5 | 6 | 7 | 8 | 9 |
|---|---|---|---|---|---|---|---|
| + 1 | + 2 | + 3 | + 4 | + 5 | + 6 | + 7 | + 8 |

To subtract with these facts, we think, "Almost all, but not quite, are taken away. Therefore, I always have one left over."

Associa-Flash Cards: (pink cards)

| 2 | 3 | 4 | 5 | 6 | 7 | 8 | 9 |
|---|---|---|---|---|---|---|---|
| − 1 | − 2 | − 3 | − 4 | − 5 | − 6 | − 7 | − 8 |

Develop with the child the observation and establish the concept that in adding with 9's the answer is one less than it would be if he were adding with tens.

In subtraction, the answer is one more than with tens, or one more than the number in the ones column from which the nine is being taken. (Use either or both concepts, depending upon which is more meaningful to the child.) For this and other subtraction sets, see Teens Trick, next lesson.

$$10 \rightarrow 9$$
$$\left.\begin{array}{r} +2 \\ \hline 10 \end{array} \quad \begin{array}{r} +2 \\ \hline 11 \end{array}\right) -1$$

$$\left.\begin{array}{r} 12 \\ -10 \\ \hline 2 \end{array} \quad \begin{array}{r} 12 \\ -9 \\ \hline 3 \end{array}\right) +1$$

KEY card

**Associa-Flash cards: (yellow)**

| 9 | 9 | 9 | 9 | 9 | 9 | 9 | 9 | 2 | 3 |
|---|---|---|---|---|---|---|---|---|---|
| + 2 | + 3 | + 4 | + 5 | + 6 | + 7 | + 8 | + 9 | + 9 | + 9 |

| 11 | 12 | 13 | 14 | 15 | 16 | 17 | 18 | 19 |
|---|---|---|---|---|---|---|---|---|
| − 9 | − 9 | − 9 | − 9 | − 9 | − 9 | − 9 | − 9 | − 9 |

Working with endings: (Regrouping)

| 19 | 29 | 39 | etc. | Introduces concept of one more ten (*watch tens column move up one more.) |
|----|----|----|------|---|
| +1 | +1 | +1 | | |

| 19 | 29 | 39 | etc. | Use COUNTING FRAMES, if available, at this level to illustrate the concept involved with regrouping. |
|----|----|----|------|---|
| +2 | +3 | +4 | | |

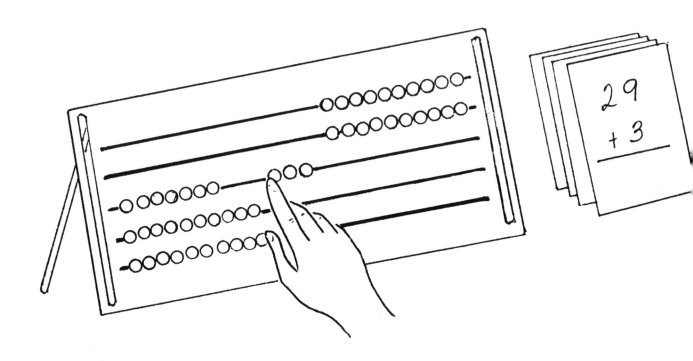

| 25 | 35 | 45 | etc. | Use of concept of thinking of one less in ones column while retaining importance of addition to tens line. |
|----|----|----|------|---|
| +9 | +9 | +9 | | |

| 25 | 35 | 45 | | Same concept, but with subtraction; child thinks one higher in ones column, while retaining importance of reducing the amount of tens. |
|----|----|----|---|---|
| − 9 | − 9 | − 9 | | |

| 33 | 26 | 54 | etc. | Once concept is established, any number added to nine can be substituted. |
|----|----|----|------|---|
| + +9 | +9 | +9 | | |

**Teens Subtraction**
**Associa-Key  orange**

Review with the children subtraction from tens. Explain that we will read our problem from left to right, so we will take eight (8) from ten (10) (not five or fifteen), and the answer is two (2).

Now, add your answer (2) to the ones place number (5). This gives us seven (7). Bring down the 7; this is the answer to our problem.

Provide practice using the key until you are sure everyone can follow the steps. The sets that make ten are provided to be sure that the first step is accurate.

| 14 | 16 | 13 | 12 | 12 | etc. any numbers |
|----|----|----|----|----|------------------|
| − 8 | − 9 | − 4 | − 3 | − 7 | |

Now, mix in numbers which look like, but do NOT require use of the teens trick (requiring only subtracting by endings).

| Examples: | 14 | 15 | 16 | 17 | 18 | 19 | etc. |
|-----------|----|----|----|----|----|----|------|
| | − 4 | − 2 | − 1 | − 5 | − 4 | − 3 | |

Practice until the child recognizes when (and how) to use his teens trick and when to subtract by endings.

Keep this key card to use regularly with math papers until no longer needed.

$$0 - 3 - 6 - 9 - 12 - 15 - 18$$
$$1 - 4 - 7 - 10 - 13 - 16 - 19$$
$$2 - 5 - 8 - 11 - 14 - 17 - 20$$

KEY card

Use as a number line

—                +

Only some students will be able to count by three's and to visualize in jumps of "three more" and "three less." For those students, introduce and practice with this set.

Associa-flash cards: (yellow)

| 1 | 2 | 3 | 4 | 5 | 6 | 7 | 8 | 9 | 3 | 3 |
|---|---|---|---|---|---|---|---|---|---|---|
| + 3 | + 3 | + 3 | + 3 | + 3 | + 3 | + 3 | + 3 | + 3 | + 3 | + 3 |

| 3 | 4 | 5 | 6 | 7 | 8 | 9 | 10 |
|---|---|---|---|---|---|---|---|
| − 3 | − 3 | − 3 | − 3 | − 3 | − 3 | − 3 | − 3 |

Working with endings:

| 13 | 14 | 15 | 16 | |
|---|---|---|---|---|
| + 3 | + 3 | + 3 | + 3 | Continued as desired with high tens. |

| 13 | 14 | 15 | 16 | 17 | 18 | 19 | |
|---|---|---|---|---|---|---|---|
| − 3 | − 3 | − 3 | − 3 | − 3 | − 3 | − 3 | Use teens trick below 13. |

$$
\begin{array}{lcccccccc}
5 & 5 & 5 & 5 & 5 & 5 & 5 & 5 & 5 \\
+1 & +2 & +3 & +4 & +5 & +6 & +7 & +8 & +9 \\
 & & & & & 11 & 12 & 13 &
\end{array}
$$

front

$$5 \quad 10 \quad 15 \quad 20 \quad 25 \quad 30 \quad etc.$$

$$+ \longrightarrow \qquad\qquad \overset{-}{\longleftarrow}$$

back

The inverse relationship of numbers shows us that we know the combinations of 1's, 2's, (3's), 9's, and doubles, and one less than the double; so we really have only 3 combinations of five to memorize. (Front of key.)

Associa-flash set:

$$
\begin{array}{cccccccccc}
5 & 5 & 5 & 5 & 5 & 5 & 5 & 5 & 2 & 3 \\
+2 & +3 & +4 & +5 & +6 & +7 & +8 & +9 & +5 & +5 \quad \text{etc.}
\end{array}
$$

$$
\begin{array}{cccc}
7 & 8 & 9 & 10 \\
-5 & -5 & -5 & -5
\end{array}
\qquad \text{Use Teens Trick for numbers beyond this point.}
$$

Most children can count by five easily, but must be shown that counting by five is the same as adding with fives. (Refer to back of key.)

$$
\begin{array}{cccccccc}
10 & 15 & 20 & 25 & 30 & 40 & 45 & 50 \\
+5 & +5 & +5 & +5 & +5 & +5 & +5 & +5
\end{array}
\qquad \text{etc. to 100;}
$$

Repeat for subtraction.

97

The concept of inverse relationship must be reinforced to develop the idea that there is less to be learned because we already know 1's, 2's, 3's, 9's, doubles, and one less than the double. We now also have learned the remaining 5's. Each associa-flash card key hereafter requires less memorization as visualized by the reduction of answers supplied on the key card. (Present sets in order as outlined.)

(It might be necessary to put the answer for each double, if this is not yet automatic for the student.)

The same keys are used for subtraction practice. Emphasize the concept of the "missing number" from the addition set, as developed in Phase No. 1 for number facts through 10.

Associa-Keys:

The student must ALWAYS have his key to which to refer as he works with his color coded flash card sets. Error-free practice is essential to reinforce positive responses only.

$\pm 4$ (blue)

| | 4 | 4 | 4 | 4 | 4 | 4 | 4 | 4 | 4 |
|---|---|---|---|---|---|---|---|---|---|
| + | 1 | 2 | 3 | 4 | 5 | 6 | 7 | 8 | 9 |
| | | | | | | 10 | 11 | 12 | |

$\pm 6$ (green)

| | 6 | 6 | 6 | 6 | 6 | 6 | 6 | 6 | 6 |
|---|---|---|---|---|---|---|---|---|---|
| + | 1 | 2 | 3 | 4 | 5 | 6 | 7 | 8 | 9 |
| | | | | | | | 13 | 14 | |

$\pm 7$ (white)

| | 7 | 7 | 7 | 7 | 7 | 7 | 7 | 7 | 7 |
|---|---|---|---|---|---|---|---|---|---|
| + | 1 | 2 | 3 | 4 | 5 | 6 | 7 | 8 | 9 |
| | | | | | | | | 15 | |

$\pm 3$ ( blue)

| | 8 | 8 | 8 | 8 | 8 | 8 | 8 | 8 | 8 |
|---|---|---|---|---|---|---|---|---|---|
| + | 1 | 2 | 3 | 4 | 5 | 6 | 7 | 8 | 9 |

| 4 | 4 | 4 | 4 | 4 | 4 | 4 | 4 | 2 | 3 |
|---|---|---|---|---|---|---|---|---|---|
| + 2 | + 3 | + 4 | + 5 | + 6 | + 7 | + 8 | + 9 | + 4 | + 4 |

Associa-Flash cards: Use appropriate colors as above.

| 5 | 6 | 7 | 8 | 9 | 10 | |
|---|---|---|---|---|---|---|
| − 4 | − 4 | − 4 | − 4 | − 4 | − 4 | Use teens trick for numbers beyond this point. |

# "Associa-Math" Program

# Phase No. 3
# Multiplication

Materials: Associa-Flash Card Set C.

Procedure:

Give each child a set of flash cards, as illustrated. A progressive presentation of multiplication facts using meaningful clues to recall (association key card and color coding) is again used to develop a constant positive automatic response to symbol recall. Present in the order given on the following pages.

The use of the Associa-Key which accompanies each flash set insures constant positive reinforcement as opposed to trial and error drill. Remember to:

1. Instruct the student to, "Take out your key card(s) and place it (them) at the top of your paper. Shuffle your flash card set(s) and place them at the left side of your work paper. Write each problem and its answer on your paper. Always refer to your key(s) so that you get the correct answer every time." (This can be for daily independent classroom time or for homework.)

2. Start with X2 (for one week of daily practice as above.) Add X5 the 2nd week. Add X9 the 3rd week. Remove X2 and add doubles. Continue adding and removing sets until all sets are completed. Never work with more (or less) than 3 sets combined. If necessary, place key cards across the room, so that the student has to get up to find the answer to his problem and hold that answer until back at his seat.

The color coding shows relationships, as well as makes it easier to shift. It also makes it possible for the teacher to quickly and easily assign specific practice.

With the Associa-Flash Math set, unlimited practice is available without the use of workbooks, which have limited controlled practice pages. With flash cards shuffled and re-shuffled, the child can write his own problems time and again as needed, until reinforcement is sufficient to make delayed recall effective.

3. Practice must move quickly into context (into problems of two and three-place numbers) or transfer may not be effective from flash cards to actual work with multiplication. At first, use only numbers that will not require regrouping. After a flash set is used for one week, add to the assignment the use of that multiplication fact with 3-place problems, as illustrated. These are to be executed with the use of the key card as a reminder to the facts recall.

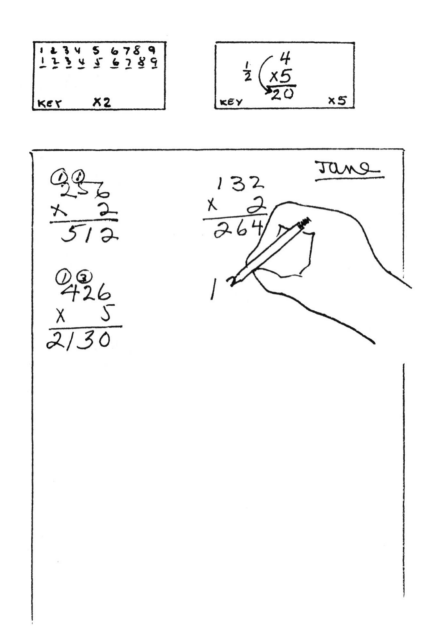

Practice must move quickly into context for transfer from flash cards to actual work to be effective. Teacher dictates problems and students can make up their own as illustrated.

1. This key is the student's reminder of the concept of X2. No answers should be needed as addition facts are supposed to be known. However, if individual students have not gained effective recall for one or two of these addition facts, his card should have those answers <u>penciled in</u>.

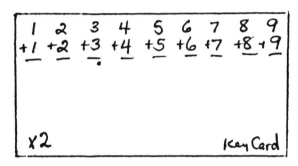

2. Associa-Flash Cards: (blue)    Practice daily for one week.

| 1 | 2 | 3 | 4 | 5 | 6 | 7 | 8 | 9 | 10 |
|---|---|---|---|---|---|---|---|---|----|
| x 2 | x 2 | x 2 | x 2 | x 2 | x 2 | x 2 | x 2 | x 2 | x 2 |

3. Then, reinforce in the context using 3-place multiplication problems. Flash cards are initial practice only, to insure concept of key card. Teacher or children can now make up problems to be solved. (Continue to refer to key card.)

(Use a directional arrow if necessary to establish right-left working habits needed for multiplication.)

←

| 11 | 12 | 13 | 14 |
|----|----|----|----|
| x 2 | x 2 | x 2 | x 2 |

(Do not go beyond 4 in ones column until regrouping has been reviewed, next page.)

| 21 | 82 | 63 | 44 |
|----|----|----|----|
| x 2 | x 2 | x 2 | x 2 |

(Continue to change number in tens column, and make up all sorts of 3-place problems.)

| 243 | 624 |
|-----|-----|
| x 2 | x 2 |

NAME _____

DATE _____

MATH
Multiplication - Division

(Grids labeled with place values: 100, 10, 1)

## Place Value

For some children, directionality or place value concepts may be the cause of errors, rather than a failure to know their multiplication tables.

Emphasis has been placed on left-right directionality in reading and writing. The child must work his multiplication from right to left, and he forgets. A directional arrow can often correct this problem.

An awareness of the concept of place value and how it relates to the multiplication problem he is attacking is also needed. Often the student will know his flash cards, but fail to transfer knowledge in double and triple place problems.

Expanded notation illustrates, in symbols, the concept of place value. Unfortunately, many children cannot "see" the relationship between the expanded visualization and the initial problem.

Lined paper turned on its side can be effectively used to work problems of multiplication or division in which placement of numbers and the reminder of place value is important to success. Or, special lined paper as illustrated above can be dittoed for use.

Have the child verbalize as he works his problem and place his answer in the proper column (writing the number from left to right):

Say:
"Five times 5 =

Five times 20 =

Five times 200 =

Now add."

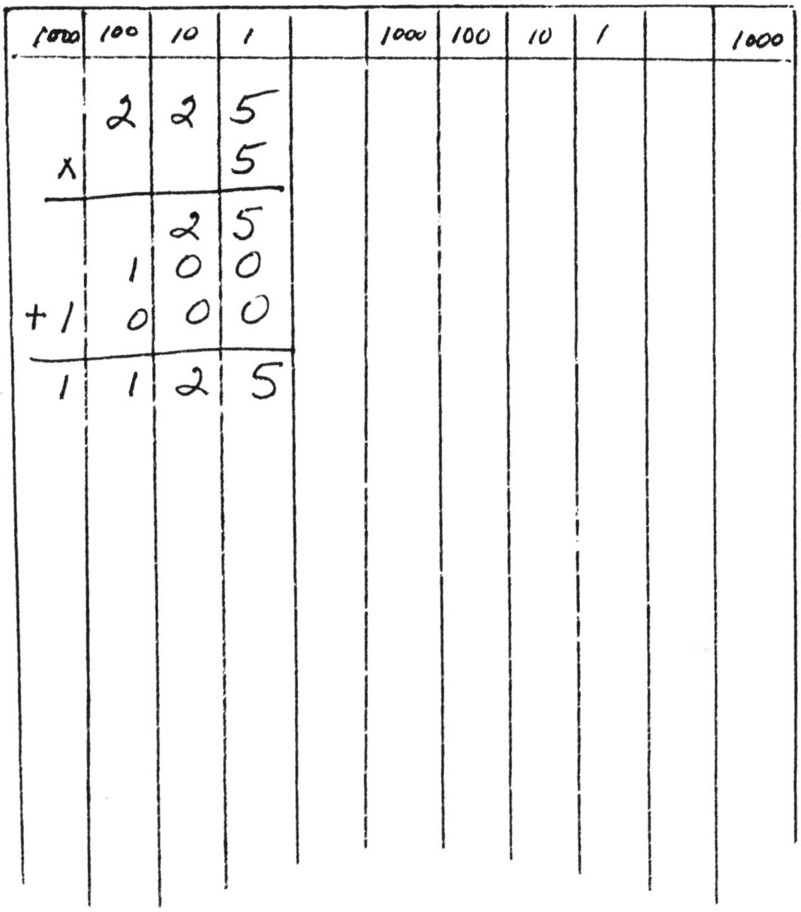

| 1000 | 100 | 10 | 1 | | 1000 | 100 | 10 | 1 | | 1000 |
|---|---|---|---|---|---|---|---|---|---|---|
| | 2 | 2 | 5 | | | | | | | |
| X | | | 5 | | | | | | | |
| | | 2 | 5 | | | | | | | |
| | 1 | 0 | 0 | | | | | | | |
| +1 | 0 | 0 | 0 | | | | | | | |
| 1 | 1 | 2 | 5 | | | | | | | |

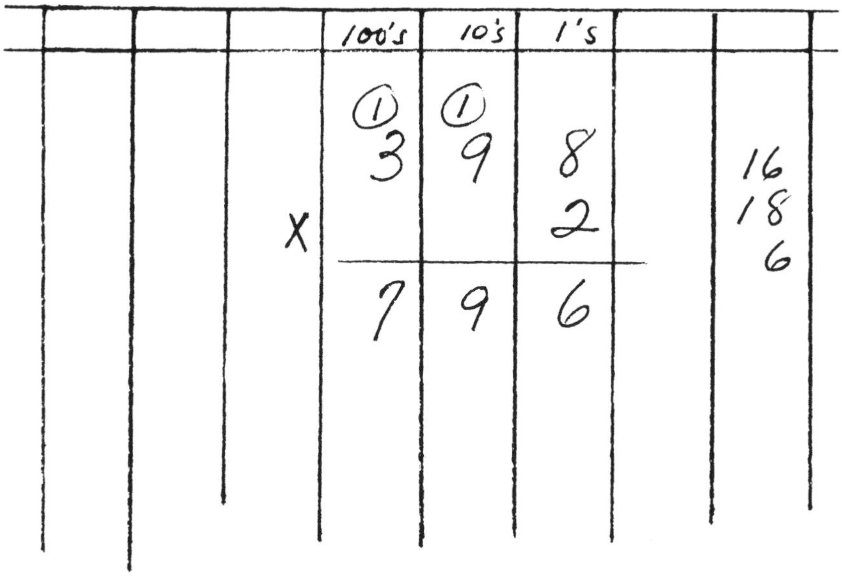

| | | | | 100's | 10's | 1's | | | |
|---|---|---|---|---|---|---|---|---|---|
| | | | | ③3 | ①9 | 8 | | 16 | |
| | | X | | | | 2 | | 18 | |
| | | | | 7 | 9 | 6 | | 6 | |

When this process is fully established, say, "Let me show you a shorter way to work. If we hold the numbers to be added at the top of the next column, we can add them as we go. Use a circle as a 'holder.'"

Continue to verbalize correctly and to write the answer at the side in order to avoid carrying the wrong part of the number, which is a very common error.

103

1. Use any ten manipulative objects to illustrate odd and even.
   a. Find "half of" with even amounts to ten. Write the number representing the quantity as you divide the piles evenly in half. Show no remainder as zero.
   b. Then find "half of" with odd amounts.

2. Discuss base 10 using fingers to explain that we made our number system to match our ten fingers. Thus, half of them is five, so "when we divide our remaining quantity in half, we will call it 5."

**Associa-Key   X5 (orange)**

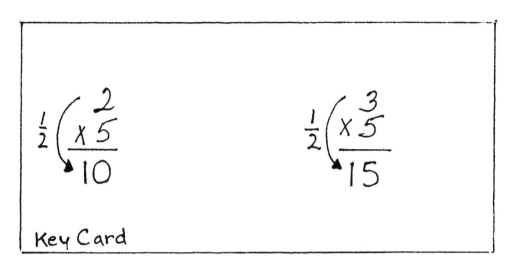

Key Card

The key card above reminds us of the trick that, "Any number multiplied by 5, think half of that number. Write this answer in the <u>tens place</u>. If multiplying an even number, put zero in the ones place, if multiplying an odd number, put 5 in the ones place."

**Associa-Flash Cards: (orange)**

Practice, then mix with X2, so the student has to shift between two "tricks," (never mix until the student understands and can use the key card).

| 1 | 2 | 3 | 4 | 5 | 6 | 7 | 8 | 9 |
|---|---|---|---|---|---|---|---|---|
| x 5 | x 5 | x 5 | x 5 | x 5 | x 5 | x 5 | x 5 | x 5 |

Optional: Show that the principle of 1/2 with 5's remains true for higher numbers.

½⟨  
| 12 | 14 | 16 | 18 | 20 | 22 | 24 | 26 | |
|---|---|---|---|---|---|---|---|---|
| x5 | x 5 | x 5 | x 5 | x 5 | x 5 | x 5 | x 5 | etc. |
60

3.  After one week, practice X5 with problems containing three-place numbers.

Example:     342
            x 5

Continue to refer to the key card.

$$9: \quad \begin{array}{l} 8+1 \\ 7+2 \\ 6+3 \\ 5+4 \end{array}$$

$$-1 \Big( \begin{array}{c} 4 \\ x\ 9 \\ \hline 3 + \triangle = 9 \end{array}$$

Key Card

1. Teach the trick, "For any number multiplied by a 9, think: 'one less than that number' (put this in the tens place). Now think: 'What added to that number ( ? ) will give me 9?' (Put this answer in the ones place.)" The factors of 9 are on the key card for reference, if needed.

2. Illustrate how this principle remains true for all the 9's and let the key card remind the pupil of the rule as he works with his flash cards.

Associa-Flash Cards (yellow)
Practice, then mix with X2 and X5 to be sure student can shift from one concept to another.

| 1 | 2 | 3 | 4 | 5 | 6 | 7 | 8 | 9 | 10 |
|---|---|---|---|---|---|---|---|---|----|
| x 9 | x 9 | x 9 | x 9 | x 9 | x 9 | x 9 | x 9 | x 9 | x 9 |

3. After one week, present three-place problems X9. Example: 236 etc. to.
$$\phantom{xxxx} \text{x  9}$$

Remember to continue to use the key card.

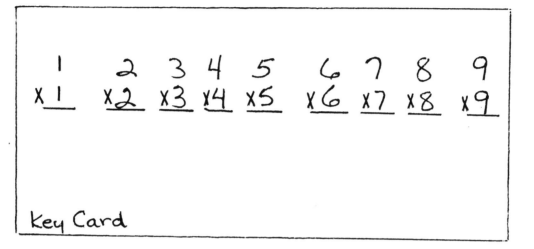

Doubles have to be memorized, but this does not seem to be difficult to do. Remind the students that they already know X1, X2, X5, X9. At first, place the answers to others than these four, in pencil, on the key card. Erase each set as learned until no answers remain.


Associa-Flash Cards (blue)

1       2       3       4       5       6       7       8       9
x 1     x 2     x 3     x 4     x 5     x 6     x 7     x 8     x 9

Reinforce the concept of the commutative property of numbers. Show the child that fewer and fewer facts have to be "learned." "You know by now your X1, X2, X5, X9 and doubles. Now, let's see what we don't know of the following tables." (It seems to come as a surprise that only a few number facts are new in each subsequent table.)

**Associa-Keys**

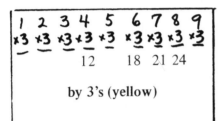

by 3's (yellow)

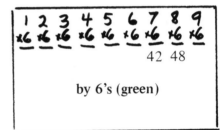

by 6's (green)

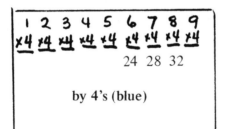

by 4's (blue)

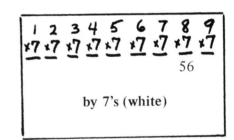

by 7's (white)

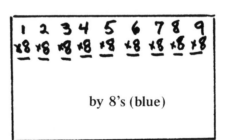

by 8's (blue)

Flash cards <u>for each set</u> are needed as illustrated below with 3's:

| 1 | 2 | 3 | 4 | 5 | 6 | 7 | 8 | 9 |
|---|---|---|---|---|---|---|---|---|
| x 3 | x 3 | x 3 | x 3 | x 3 | x 3 | x 3 | x 3 | x 3 |

(Remember to take one new table a week. Later, combine any tables for continued practice where individual differences require specific additional reinforcement.)

# Associa-Math Program

## Phase No. 3
## Division

<u>Materials:</u> Associa-Flash Card Set $C_2$

<u>Procedure:</u> Give a set of color coded Associa-Math Flash Cards with keys, as illustrated in the following pages, to each student for controlled, error-free practice to reinforce automatic auditory and visual recall of division facts. Present in the order given on the following pages.

1.  Instruct the student to, "Take out your key card(s) and place it (them) at the top of your paper. Shuffle the flash card set (s) and place them at the left of your work paper. Write each problem and its answer. Be sure to use your keys as a recall aid so that all your answers are correct."

2.  Practice with the first set for one week. Now, add the second set and practice both mixed together for another week. Add a third set and mix. The next week, remove one set, then add one set. Continue in this manner until all sets have been studied.

3.  Practice must move quickly into the context of normal use. After a week's practice with a controlled flash card set, problems with three-place dividends should be given (but divisor controlled and key card used to assure correct number fact responses.

**Associa-Key (blue)**          **Division by 2's**

| 1 | 2 | 3 | 4 | 5 | 6 | 7 | 8 | 9 |
|---|---|---|---|---|---|---|---|---|
| $+1$ | $+2$ | $+3$ | $+4$ | $+5$ | $+6$ | $+7$ | $+8$ | $+9$ |
| 2 | 4 | 6 | 8 | 10 | 12 | 14 | 16 | 18 |

Even $\quad 2\overline{)\square}\;^{½}$ $\qquad\qquad$ Odd $\quad 2\overline{)\square}\;^{½}$ R1

Introduce the concept of $\div 2$ as one half of a set of items. Illustrate with manipulative items and write the quantities as you divide.
Introduce key card above as reminder of doubles sets.

**Associa-Flash Cards: (blue)**

From the beginning it is essential to use the full division process as illustrated.

$$2\overline{)2} \quad \begin{array}{r} 1 \\ \hline \phantom{2} \\ 2 \\ \hline 0 \end{array}$$

$$\begin{array}{r} 2 \\ 2\overline{)4} \\ 4 \\ \hline 0 \end{array} \qquad 2\overline{)6} \qquad 2\overline{)8}$$

From 10 on, reinforce place value, and be sure the answer is placed over the ones part of the number. This is essential for later progress.

$$\begin{array}{r} 5 \\ 2\overline{)10} \\ 10 \\ \hline 0 \end{array} \qquad 2\overline{)10} \quad 2\overline{)12} \quad 2\overline{)14} \quad 2\overline{)16} \quad 2\overline{)18} \quad 2\overline{)20}$$

Explain uneven sets and show students how to record remainders before presenting these cards. Print odd dividends in red. Mix sets.

$$\begin{array}{r} 1 \text{ R1}\\ 2\overline{)3} \\ 2 \\ \hline 1 \end{array} \quad 2\overline{)5} \quad 2\overline{)7} \quad 2\overline{)9} \quad 2\overline{)11} \quad 2\overline{)13} \quad 2\overline{)15} \quad 2\overline{)17} \quad 2\overline{)19} \quad 2\overline{)21}$$

After one week of controlled practice, introduce larger numbers. Always use full division process. Teach students to look for "units" as in the last example.

$$\begin{array}{r} 123 \\ 2\overline{)246} \\ 2 \\ \hline 46 \\ 40 \\ \hline 6 \end{array} \qquad 2\overline{)482} \qquad 2\overline{)648} \qquad \begin{array}{r} 821 \text{ R1} \\ 2\overline{)1643} \\ 16 \\ \hline 43 \\ 40 \\ \hline 3 \\ 2 \\ \hline 1 \end{array}$$

Next, introduce numbers which will require a zero as place holder. Be sure the concept of units and place value is clearly established, so answers are written over in the correct place. Thus, the zero is meaningful.

$$\begin{array}{r} 708 \\ 2\overline{)1416} \\ 14 \\ \hline 16 \\ 16 \end{array}$$

```
5x   ?  =   5
     ?  =  10
     ?  =  15
     4  =  20
     5  =  25
     6  =  30
     7  =  35
     8  =  40
     9  =  45
```

The key above is the remainder of the concept of inverse relationships. Omit answers (?) if X(times) facts are well established. Insert those not yet automatic. This assures accuracy and reinforcement of multiplication facts as a part of division practice. (Concept for remainder is constant regardless of number in tens place.)


Associa-Flash Cards Set (orange)

1. Evenly divisible problems. Use long division process at all times.

$5\overline{)5}$   $5\overline{)10}$   $5\overline{)15}$   $5\overline{)20}$   $5\overline{)25}$   $5\overline{)30}$   $5\overline{)35}$   $5\overline{)40}$   $5\overline{)45}$

2. Use this set only after set above is practiced and understood. (Where remainders are to be expected, put the dividend in red.)

$5\overline{)6}$   $5\overline{)7}$   $5\overline{)8}$   $5\overline{)9}$   etc. through 49, omitting evenly divisible numbers.

Remember, after one week of practice, work in multi-figure dividends.

111

The concept and realization of inverse relationships must be taught to lead the student to understand that fewer facts have to be learned as he gets each new set. ALWAYS USE THE KEY CARD to insure positive error-free practice.

Associa-Keys:

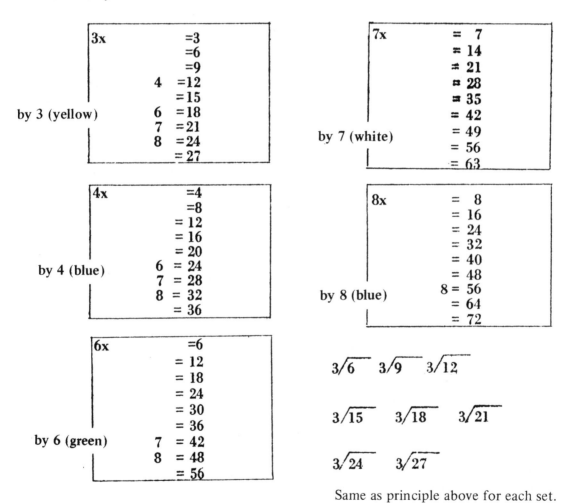

$3\overline{)6}$   $3\overline{)9}$   $3\overline{)12}$

$3\overline{)15}$   $3\overline{)18}$   $3\overline{)21}$

$3\overline{)24}$   $3\overline{)27}$

Same as principle above for each set.

112

# Chapter IV
# THE CLASSROOM SETTING

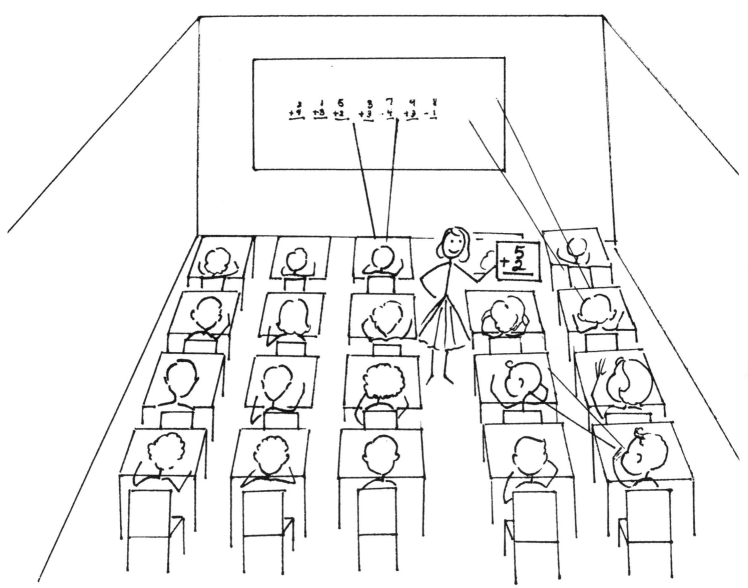

GENERAL PRINCIPLES FOR GROUP TEACHING

I. SEATING

Children with perceptual or motor lags need close contact with the teacher and the materials. They are not children who can be easily controlled with voice only. A reward system is a positive and useful addition to motivation, but <u>in itself,</u> will not keep his attention. Rewards can be used — but as additional motivators — and used in moderation, so that the effect is more lasting.

Some children are easily distracted. At times such children can have catastrophic reactions to another child in the room or to activities which are too stimulating. Thus, a quiet, well controlled, structured classroom environment is essential for him.

Specific seating patterns for use with small groups are attached.

Several general principles apply for all seating patterns:

The children with perceptual problems must be close enough to the board and in front of it, so that perceptual difficulty is minimized. Preferably they should copy from work on their desk, as distance from copy increases errors.

Children need to be in close proximity to the teacher, so that at any given moment she can reach out and physically contact the student. The teacher should work among the children while she presents material. The closer the physical contact, the better the attention ability of the child. Miniature chalkboard carried by the teacher should be used, rather than the room board which is often too distant.

While children are working on an assignment, the teacher should always be observing and helping from behind the group. This way, the teacher has visual contact with all of the papers and can correct mistakes as or before they are made, so that positive reinforcement is established during the lesson. The teacher is also able to head-off possible discipline or attention problems as or before they evolve. By circulating from behind, the teacher is less likely to distract the working pupils.

## II. ACTIVITIES

A. Many children do best in a group when they are actively and kinesthetically involved in the work. Attention may be lost and discipline can become a problem if children are required to sit very still while the teacher pursues a lesson through lecture fashion.

B. Verbiage should be of a minimum. Instructions must be clear and short.

C. A routine should be established and followed so that the children know exactly what to expect. Repetitive activities and approaches give security, allowing them to put their attention and effort on the lesson or activity.

D. A minimum of materials should be available at one time. Pencils, notebooks, other items NOT IN USE for the lesson become a distraction. If desks are clear of all things not needed in the specific activity, work will progress more satisfactorily. DO NOT give out materials before they are needed or the children may be playing with them while instructions are being given. Give materials with specific instruction as to their use at that moment.

E. Lessons must be carefully planned, so that the group will begin work as soon as they come into a room. In this way, attention is captured and directed to a specific activity before a breakdown in attention can occur from hyperactivity and distractibility. Any lapse of time, where activity is non-directed, can lose these children.

F. Something should be provided to keep their hands and minds busy, if there is a waiting period between activities. This can be erector sets stored in shoe boxes and composed of nuts and bolts and pegboard pieces, or sets such as "Multi-Fit", "Jumbo Lego," or "Snap-N-Play Blocks" (available from CHILDCRAFT, Edison, New Jersey).

## SEATING SUGGESTIONS FOR GROUPS

(Key for small group seating)

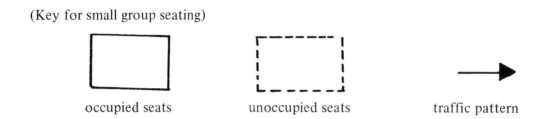

occupied seats          unoccupied seats          traffic pattern

      Classrooms of 20-30 students should be broken into two sections. While one group is instructed, the other does completely independent activities requiring no guidance and at a level suitable, so that errors in work are not likely to occur. All types of drill, practice, tracing, and other reinforcement activities should be used by the inactive half of the class. The working half will be doing instructional work which requires close supervision. In this way, teacher time is utilized to the fullest so that pupils during a learning activity have success and adequate guidance, yet reinforcement independent work does not keep the teacher inactive with the children.

Grouping where NO board is needed:

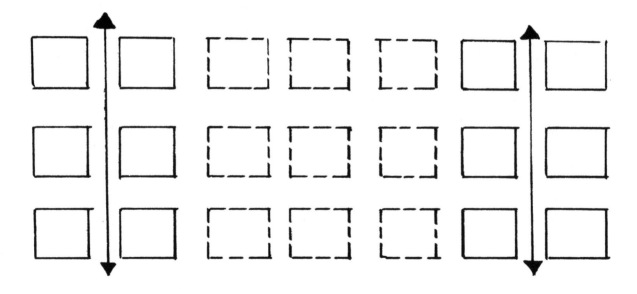

Grouping where board is to be used:

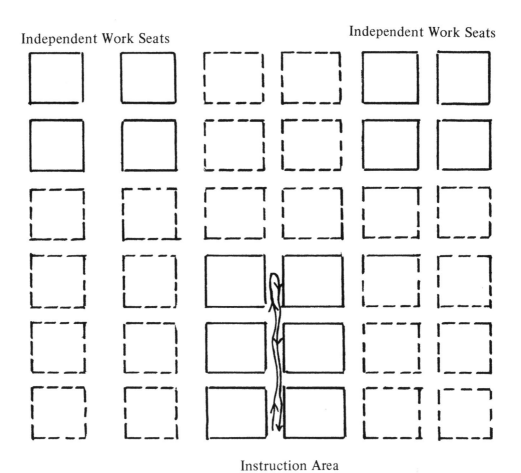

Independent Work Seats

Independent Work Seats

Instruction Area

## STANDARDIZED TESTING

I. Standardized Tests must be given in a uniform manner following the specific administrative instructions in the manuals. However, the verbiage of most standardized tests loses many children. Children with perceptual problems may not understand what to do as they need an example rather than verbal instructions.

Where distractibility, hyperactivity, and unstructured environment become a major factor in teaching or testing, certain additional test procedures are suggested.

A. Test in groups of 8 – 10 in order to temper the possibility of other children acting as a catalyst and disturbing the necessary calm and attention to the task at hand, and to the examiner giving instructions or test parts which need to be read.

If it is not possible to test in small groups, groups up to 20 may be formed by having them in one classroom but divided somewhat into two sets with an examiner's aid to each set.

B. Have the test room cleared of distracting material. Do not allow the children to bring anything with them to the test room. Do not provide pencils or test booklets until children are ready to begin.

C. Provide a planned seating arrangement according to knowledge of pupil needs.

D. Prepare the children immediately upon entering the room for the purpose of their presence and as to the exact procedure to be followed in preparation. (Tension from uncertainty and unstructured, unfamiliar situation can cause it to be hard to settle the testees and may cause a negative response to the test itself.)

E. Avoid answering questions until everyone is settled and has been given instructions. Then accept pertinent questions.

F. Do not allow children to get out of their seat. Go to them if necessary.

G. Examiner should avoid disturbing the children by talking with examiner's helper. Those helping in the test situation should stand at the back of the room to avoid being noticed by the children in his observation of them.

H. Tester should speak in a clear, authoritative voice which commands attention from the child with a short attention span. The pace must be fast enough to keep their attention, yet clear enough to make it unnecessary to repeat or explain any instructions.

I. Make sure the students are keeping their place and show them what to do whenever needed.

J. Be sure they don't stop and stare off into space. Keep encouraging them to move on.

L. Make careful notes of the behavior during testing, so the end score will be valid. For example:

      1. Watch to see if the students work randomly just to get finished.

      2. Do they need directions illustrated?

      3. Can they read the words (on vocabulary tests)?

      4. Do they copy their neighbor?

      5. Do they lose their place?

At appropriate places, it is important to stop for a <u>very brief</u> break in the test. Use this break as a bathroom break, or ask pupils to stand by their chair and perform a few simple exercises at tester's suggestion. Do not allow a free period break. Any break which is too long or too stimulating may destroy the calm atmosphere so vital to a successful test situation.

# Glossary

## associative approach

addition of a meaningful clue to a symbol which in itself has no clue to its meaning. The purpose is to evoke recall for the symbol.

## auditory:kinesthetic match

involves a say-and-do or a hear-and-do activity.

## auditory:visual match

accurately attaching an auditory (sound or word) stimulus with its visual referent (object or symbol).

## body awareness

an automatic, unconscious ability to move through space.

## deficit

a defect, imperfection, or an inadequacy.

## developmental lag

a slower rate or a delay in development (but not a deficit).

## directional awareness

an automatic and unconscious knowledge of direction or relationship of objects to self and to each other. Refers to leftness and rightness, upness and downness with objects and symbols, and to geographic awareness and being able to find your way around in new places.

## discrimination (visual) (auditory)

ability to (see) (hear) the likeness or difference between (objects) (sounds) and/or symbols.

## eye:hand coordination

smooth and coordinated movement of the hand guiding the eye (in pointing) or the eye guiding the hand (in writing). A matching of two motor systems to perform one function.

## figure:ground perception

the ability to focus on and pull to the fore pertinent details from a background or group of details. Example: 1) seeing "Mother" in a crowd of people; 2) finding a word on a page of words.

## Key Card

a visually static stimulus that offers a meaningful clue to aid part-to-whole perception and recall

## "Kina-Bingo"

a variation of the game Bingo, devised by the authors that requires a kinesthetic action in playing the game of Bingo.

**"Kina-Writing"**
a term coined by the authors for their development of a method of visual-auditory-Associative tracing, used to reinforce cursive style, vocabulary meaning and recognition and spelling.

**kinesthetic**
learning through movement about ourselves and our environment; measures received through the muscular system.

**learning mode**
manner, style, or method by which a person gains knowledge about his environment; a pattern of strengths and weaknesses.

**manipulative materials**
three-dimensional materials that can be handled and moved about. Used in learning form, size, sequencing, spatial relationships, and in intensifying data to pull a figure from its background.

**part-to-whole**
ability to place details (pieces) in correct relationships to each other, so that a meaningful total is obtained therefrom.

**perceptual constancy (visual) (auditory)**
recognition of an image (or sound) as being the same image (or sound) when seen (heard) again, either in the same circumstances, position, etc., or in different surroundings at a different time.

**perceptually impaired**
an inability to make (adequate) meaning from presented stimuli.

**pictograms**
use of pictures in place of words to communicate information

**rote learner**
one who memorizes or repeats information in a mechanical way without attention to basic principles, concepts, rules or meaning.

**sound/symbol association**
sound unit and its symbol referent(s); must be closely and meaningfully associated with each other for recall: in spelling, sound to symbol, and in reading, symbol to sound.

**static visual referent**
visual presentation which remains present for viewing while working; non-moving object or symbol.

### three-dimensional (3-D)

having the properties of height, width and thickness. With these properties objects are easier to "see" and can be handled and manipulated.

### visual function

the use or performance of the eyes in gathering information about the environment. The way the eyes operate.

### visualization

the ability to form a mental image form previously experienced stimuli.

### visual:motor coordination

see eye:hand

### visual skills

the effective or proficient use of the eyes in gathering information about the environment.

### word analysis

the breaking down of words into their parts in order to identify the word. Phonetic approach (as opposed to sight recognition) to decoding a word.

* * * * * * * * * * * * *

# ABOUT THE AUTHORS

*Norma Banas is president and director of curriculum of Educational Guidance Services, Inc. She received her B.Ed. in secondary education in 1957, and her M.Ed. in clinical reading in 1965, both from the University of Miami. Her work experience has led her from the classroom to the University of Miami Reading Clinic, to curriculum director of the McGlannan School for five years, and to her present association with EGS.*

Norma Banas

I. H. Wills

*Isabel Wills is secretary-treasurer and diagnostic director of Educational Guidance Services, Inc., in Miami, Florida. She did her undergraduate work at the University of Pittsburgh, received her M.S. in psychology from the University of Miami, and has had postgraduate training in clinical reading and neuropsychology. Mrs. Wills worked in the area of evaluation at the University of Miami, in private practice, and as diagnostic director for the McGlannan School before becoming co-founder of EGS in 1967.*

*Mrs. Banas and Mrs. Wills established Educational Guidance Services, Inc. as an organization dedicated to developing learning strengths through prescriptive educational programming. Their objective is to provide students with the tools for learning as they feel that the worst thing we can do as parents or as teachers is to make students dependent on us. Mrs. Banas and Mrs. Wills have been recognized for their work with children by Who's Who in American Women, among other biographies. They are contributing editors, since 1968, to the journal, Academic Therapy. They have co-authored several texts and prescriptive teaching guides, write for many journals, contribute to conferences and conduct workshops all over the south.*

127

Printed in Great Britain
by Amazon

17461491R00081